Seven Keys to Happiness

Don J. Black

Brigham Young
University
Publications

Library of Congress Catalog Card Number: 74-186681
International Standard Book Number: 0-8425-1451-1
Brigham Young University Publications, Provo, Utah 84601
© 1972 by Brigham Young University Publications. All rights reserved
Printed in the United States of America
72 10M 98660

*To my lovely wife, my best
friend and companion.
Because of her continual example
and application of unceasing
love, humor, understanding,
and deep spiritual influence,
my life is most richly blessed
with great happiness.
Thank you, Ann.*

Table of Contents

Preface

This writing is autobiographical. In no way does it attempt to reflect literary genius. It is written in lay language, and its sole purpose is to share personal experiences and ideas, with the hope that they will inspire in some small way greater happiness in the lives of others. It is also written in the spirit of prayer, with a special request made to our Father that those subjects outlined and applied will render genuine benefit in the life of the reader.

Introduction

The following letter was allegedly written by a
bricklayer to the firm he worked for.*

Respected sir:

*When I got to the building, I found that a hurri-
cane had knocked some bricks off the top. So I rigged
up a beam with a pulley at the top of the building
and hoisted up a couple of barrels full of bricks.
When I had fixed the building, there were a lot of
bricks left over. I hoisted the barrel back up again and
secured the line at the bottom, and then went up and
filled the barrel with extra bricks. Then I went to the
bottom and cast off the line. Unfortunately the barrel
of bricks was heavier than I, so before I knew what
was happening the barrel started down, jerking me off
the ground. I decided to hang on, and halfway up I
met the barrel coming down and received a severe
blow on the shoulder. I then continued to the top,
banging my head against the beam and getting my
fingers jammed in the pulley. When the barrel hit the
ground it bursted its bottom, allowing all the bricks
to spill out. I was now heavier than the barrel and
started down again at high speed. Halfway down, I
met the barrel coming up and received severe injuries
to my shins. When I hit the ground I landed on the
bricks, getting several painful cuts from sharp edges.
At this point I must have lost my presence of mind,
because I let go of the line. The barrel then came
down with great haste, giving me another heavy blow*

*Unfortunately repeated efforts have failed to disclose
the source of this letter.

*in the head, putting me in the hospital. I respectfully
request sick leave.*

Convinced there are others in this world who have
their ups and downs, or times of unhappiness? There
are. This book outlines a program of seven initial
steps for bringing greater happiness into your life.
Obviously, all information in this writing will not
apply to everyone. It is hoped some will apply to all.

The idea started a few seasons ago while my wife
and I visited the once famed hippie commune known
as Haight-Ashbury in San Francisco. We went with
the intention of learning more about youth problems,
causes of unhappiness, and, maybe more specifically,
the lure of the "new movement." It was difficult to
fully determine the lure. Oh, the facade of freedom
was apparent, but this type of freedom did not seem
to emanate happiness. We saw children, many young
runaways, banging on car windows of passing curiosity seekers and tourists, begging for financial
handouts, to buy more drugs or possibly to donate to
the commune's, or "pad's," food supply of brown
rice. Many of the kids looked depressed, almost as if
the personal disappointment and failure of their
new-found life was too much to openly confess. We
noticed one young man lying on a bench, another on
the sidewalk near a park, both covered with sheets of
newspaper. It was midafternoon.

Although we looked for evidence of the newly
claimed truth and happiness, we found difficulty
deciphering it. Some had smiles, but not the radiant
smiles that begin within. We saw scabby-faced kids,
probably doing too much speed. From cases treated
at the Haight-Ashbury Free Medical Clinic, we
learned that many young people were suffering from
malnutrition, hepatitis, paranoia, and other ailments,
as a result of too much self-inflicted poison.

The whole essence of our visit really came into
focus, however, when we noticed a seemingly inno-
cent attraction upon the street at an intersection.
There, written by the city, were the accustomed

elongated letters S-T-O-P. One of the kids, desiring an addition to the message, added with white spray paint—and, I must confess, very neatly—the words, "THE WAR!"

Obviously, he referred to the Vietnam conflict, but as I gazed at the added wording and the immediate environment, a much deeper thought came to mind. Yes, the young man was correct in his additional thought reflecting international matters, but what if that same thought were applied to the mind, or the body, or the spirit? Stop the war *within*: the war with hate, the personal war with God, the cause of so much of our unhappiness—unhappiness that is so noticeable in nations, cities, even families. Wouldn't it be nice to stop the war between parents, between parents and their children, between children and their brothers and sisters, even between neighbors? Wouldn't it be nice if the word *divorce* were erased and no longer used as a common term? It seems when young married couples today have a squabble one of the first things that comes to mind is divorce. Wouldn't it be swell to see happiness begin to come back into families, cities, and nations, bringing with it that special radiance of inner warmth, almost contagious if sincerely given the chance.

To gain such happiness requires many things. Seven, found through serious study coupled with experience, will be discussed in this book. Together with these seven, it is also important and somewhat consoling to know that the person seeking additional happiness in life is not alone in his position. Strange as it may seem, the beginning of comfort and happiness often comes from the knowledge that many others are and have been in unfavorable circumstances, causing them various degrees of unhappiness, but have overcome the difficulties.

Our greatest government, athletic, and religious leaders have had their share of unhappiness at one time or another. For a moment, take a look at our great president, Abraham Lincoln. His record is sorrowfully fascinating! He failed in business in 1831.

He was defeated for state legislature in 1832. In
1833 he failed in business again. He was elected for
legislature in 1834, defeated for Speaker of the
House in 1838, defeated for elector in 1840, and
defeated for Congress in 1843. He was elected to
Congress later and defeated for Congress again in
1848. He was defeated for Senate in 1855. He was
defeated in 1856 for vice-president, and later in 1858
for Senate. With defeats come unhappiness, but that
unhappiness should not necessarily be permanent.
The great Mr. Lincoln used the defeats as guidelines
to better himself and hit the challenging task harder
next time, forcing himself to find the happiness
originally sought after but temporarily lost.

It is said that the renowned Babe Ruth's record is
symbolic of great athletic achievement. Ruth is still
the idol of baseball players nationwide, but he holds
one record few know about. The great Babe struck
out more times than any other player in history—a
price he had to pay in setting other records, a price
most valuable, for it rendered unto him great experience and, eventually, great happiness.

The great and beloved young prophet Joseph
Smith took his share of unhappiness while on this
earth. Maybe you recall his several incarcerations—
particularly his imprisonment in the Richmond Jail
and his gross unhappiness with the fiendish boasts of
his guards. That was the time he stood in chains
behind bars and, unable to bear the obscenities any
longer, rebuked the guards, warning them they had
better cease their vile speaking. He had a wife and
family during these times.

Another time he was confined to the Liberty Jail,
also referred to by some as the Liberty Temple, for
from this dungeon President Smith led the activities
of the church and within its barren and cold walls
received several great revelations. That was the long,
cold winter of 1838 and 1839. In March of 1839
Joseph received one of the most powerful revelations
from God to man. It concerned persecution, trial, and
unhappiness. Joseph was very unhappy with the

treatment of his family, the Saints, and himself by the mobs, and reminded the Lord of the Saints' hardships and sorrows. This sorrowful, yet spiritually fascinating, passage changes from prayer (section 121, verses 1-6) to direct and divine intervention by revelation. The Lord reveals to Joseph various forms of unhappiness, and at the last of section 122 tells Joseph the reason for trials and unhappiness. The Lord explains that man must experience some unhappiness or bitterness in life to appreciate and recognize the sweet and good. He emphasizes that trials and some unhappiness are actually for man's good.

Never has the Lord, however, condoned continual unhappiness. Hence the many aids given to man for building and maintaining happiness: e.g., music, poetry, stories, exemplary lives, nature, the scriptures, good books. The content of *Seven Keys to Happiness* was originally presented as lectures, given numerous times to various types of audiences. Response received in most cases was very positive. The ideas contained herein are the very keys and secrets I have personally tried throughout my own life. It is sincerely hoped these same ideas will help others in their quest for greater happiness and appreciation of life.

One must not overlook, however, that happiness translated into deeper meaning includes challenge. It is a commodity requiring action, self-discipline, and sincere giving of oneself. For the seeker of happiness the world offers a great variety of opportunities to meet this end. An unknown but perceptive author has given us a fresh overview of the opportunities, challenges, and sacrifices about us.

God left the world unfinished, for man to work his skill upon.
He left the oil still in the earth, the electricity still in the clouds.
He left the rivers unbridged, the forests unfelled, the cities unbuilt.

God gave to man the challenge of raw materials, not
    the ease of finished things.
He left the music unsung and the pictures unpainted
    and the problems unsolved.
That man might know the joys and glories of creation,
    God also left man unfinished:
He left the lessons unlearned, the testimonies
    unformed, the abilities undeveloped, that man
    might share in his own creation and in the work
    of becoming as God is.

In this inspired thought we might rightfully read
between the lines, "God left much happiness in the
world, for man to seek, then enjoy."

The main difference in people, when all is said and
done, is their happiness or their lack of it. Make yours
happiness—total happiness, both physically and
spiritually. It does make the difference.

First Key

*Know and appreciate
yourself and the world
around you.*

Know and appreciate yourself and the world around you. Get to know both the good and the bad in yourself. Accept inherited weaknesses, and improve upon those changeable. Begin to appreciate and become sensitive to the things of life around you.

A somewhat humorous example of those things in life which are disliked but not really changeable comes from my experience as a young boy. I was greatly aware of my skinny legs, and I hesitate to recall the number of rich chocolate malts I consumed, hoping to gain extra weight. I avoided all public or school swimming or athletic events which required showing of my legs. Once at a tristake beach party held at one of the familiar "Mormon" beaches in Southern California I mustered up enough courage to attend. It was to be at night, and chances were good I could hide when necessary. I recall changing my clothes to a bathing suit I already had on under my clothing, but not out in the open like the athletic type. I did it behind a nearby garbage can while all attention was focused on the muscular "afters" of the body-building advertisements—the ones who didn't get the sand kicked in their faces. Then under cover of darkness, far enough away from the flickering light of the bonfire, I would enter the water alone while the others all went in together. I remember the surprised looks on a few faces when I would suddenly appear. I learned well the tricks of making myself look a bit heavier, like never facing the group straight on to reveal my bony knees, or squatting upon my legs when sitting down, causing them to appear heavier than they were.

This "thing" really started to become an obsession with me. It went on for some time until one day, while walking past a little shop, I noticed a sign which read, "You heard about the man who cried and cried because he had no shoes, until he saw the man who had no feet." Oh, did that inspired passage hit this young soul. I gave deep thought to its rich wisdom. I thought about my legs and said to myself, "You know, they do work pretty good." I could say to my

3

legs, "Let's get up and walk around a bit," and they would. Or, we could even run if we wished. I recall being about the fastest kid in our neighborhood for years. I thought of the calls in the hallway, "Hey, Birdlegs!" I recall today all too vividly kids in my classes, and their occasional remarks when I turned sideways, "Hey, he's gone. Let's go!" What did it *really* matter? My legs worked fine. Besides, I suddenly reasoned, good runners always seemed to have thin legs. Mine were thin. That's why I was a good runner. Not bad. I felt better.

A person can't do a lot about a crooked nose, blue eyes instead of brown, or the fact that he or she doesn't resemble Steve McQueen or Raquel Welch. These things we might call inherited characteristics— usually the unchangeables, the things we have to live with, whether we like it a lot or not. One of the key prerequisites of happiness is accepting that which we cannot change. About those things changeable—well, we'll talk about it in just a moment. But more about the unchangeables and how to confront them.

As in many other concerns in life, attitude again sneaks up to the front of the list of the character traits important in overcoming inherited weaknesses or concerns. (The skinny leg thing was more concern than actual weakness.) When I was about three years of age, before the days of modern vaccines, an attack of the measles affected my hearing. I recall how I first discovered the damage. The telephone rang, and as this is an exciting event in a youngster's life, I answered it. I heard nothing. My mother took the phone and said hello, and heard the loud voice of my grandmother trying to get through the suspected bad connection. I tried it again, but still could hear nothing. When my mother held the phone to my other ear, however, the message came through loud and clear. My bout with measles had damaged the ear drum of my left ear, rendering me deaf in that ear.

This sort of thing doesn't really affect the emotions or character of such a young child; so for many years nothing much was thought of it. Then sophis-

5

ticated medicine began its momentous role in the world. I read one day about delicate ear surgery, replacing a damaged ear drum and restoring hearing. This sounded exciting to me, and so I went down to an ear specialist the following day. Under closer observation, it was found that since the initial ear drum disorder the central hearing nerve had completely deteriorated. There was no hope until nerve transplants were devised—now a not-so-far-out dream, presently being studied in the medical field. I was disappointed.

When stereophonic devices came forth, people tried to explain to me the difference between it and the suddenly outdated high fidelity. Stereo sounded fascinating. How would it be to hear true stereo? It began to bother me. I thought, why do I have to go through life not really knowing where sound originates, or wondering what true, divided stereo sounds like?

I pondered upon the dilemma for quite some time off and on, and then another one of those "skinny legs" experiences took place. While doing research for a specialized college course, I had to visit a state school for handicapped children. My answer to self-pity awaited me. There I witnessed many of those sweet children who had never heard a sound in their young lives. This prevented them from verbally sounding letters and words, and thus their speech was greatly impaired. Most could not talk. I thought of my own situation. I heard perfectly well with the one ear. So I didn't have stereo. There are a lot of people who never own a Cadillac. Fords are not really that bad, I thought.

By the way, this experience gave me good reason to look forward to the resurrection. If I watched myself closely, and tried my best to be worthy, at that time I could trade in this old, outdated high fidelity outfit for an authentic stereo. I have always liked little special things to look forward to in life. This expectation would be worthwhile.

Now a word to those blessed individuals who don't

have a hearing loss or have not been endowed with the challenge of hearing such cries as "I've seen better-looking legs on a table!" There are other ways we can become sensitive to the good of ourselves. Let me illustrate a few of these methods of becoming newly aware of your personal worth and positively sensitive to what you really are and have.

While I was employed by one of California's aerospace industries, we had a young lad working for the company as a mail boy. He was a tall, handsome, blond fellow. One day, while riding his motorcycle, he apparently hit a slick spot or some obstruction in the street while turning a corner, causing the bike to go out of control, and during the fall the boy's arm became trapped under the sliding machine. Needless to say, his arm was seriously injured. Despite efforts of surgeons to save his arm, it was necessary to amputate. The operation took his arm off at his shoulder. It was his right arm; he was right-handed. We were all very saddened at this news, but happy to know he was recovering well and would soon be back on the job after a normal rehabilitation period. After some time the young man returned to his job.

I first noticed his return when we met in the men's lounge. My curiosity was very suddenly awakened, wondering how he was able to carry out the usual daily tasks required. I was washing my hands. I watched him as he washed his hand. I tore off a paper towel and dried my hands. He tore off a paper towel. I wondered how he would wipe his one hand without the assistance of the other. How would he hold the towel? I saw as he placed the towel against his chest and then, with a quick, coordinated movement, began rubbing his hand upon the towel, wiping in the best way possible. I combed my hair, using the two-hand method men usually use, though the assistance rendered by the second hand is usually not much more than psychological. But it's part of the process. I watched the young lad as he combed his hair with one hand. I tucked in my shirttails, a customary operation when refreshing at midday. I became aware

7

of my appreciation of both hands to assist me in this apparently simple task. I watched him as he tried to loosen his belt and tuck his shirttail in with one hand.

The entire experience of those few moments together with him depressed me. I thought of the many tasks executed daily needing both hands, always taken for granted: tying a shoe, zipping a zipper, buttoning a button, tying a tie, or just taking a dollar bill from your wallet. My thoughts raced with the sudden need for reappreciation. I wondered how I could print indelibly into my being this new-found need for appreciation. There must be some way to make it last a little longer than the following *hour*. I decided silently as I left the men's room I would somehow sacrifice the use of my own arm to gain that needed appreciation. I made an agreement with myself to put my hand into my pocket and not use it for the remainder of the day. Then I would know the difference, firsthand.

My experiment started without apparent sacrifice. As the day went on, however, my appreciation grew more intense. Little things like placing a dime in the soft drink machine gave no challenge; nor did the same task at the candy machine. I was serving the aerospace industry at this time as a technical writer. It required handwriting copy most of the day. I soon adjusted, though roughly, to the use of my left hand for writing, but my first forced challenge came when I broke the lead in my pencil. I walked over to the pencil sharpener and then realized my inadequacy. I tried holding the pencil and turning the handle of the sharpener simultaneously. It just didn't work. I hailed a passing colleague and asked if he would hold the pencil while I turned the handle. He obliged kindly, taking somewhat suspicious notice of my unused hand in my pocket. We finished the task and I thanked him, but he immediately asked innocently, but interestedly, "What's wrong with your hand?"

Rather than gamble for acceptance of my unusual experiment, I just looked at him with a half smile and, while slowly walking away, muttered, "Nothing, thanks." I remember the puzzled look on his face.

I suffered through the rest of the day, learning something new each moment, causing me to appreciate anew my limbs. The day was nearly ended. Oh, it would be nice voluntarily to put myself back into complete action. I was glad I had challenged myself for only a day. I walked out of the plant, determined to finish the original deal honorably. I felt assured of victory until I entered my Volkswagen. Try it, folks. It's a guaranteed method of gaining reappreciation of something all too often taken for granted. It's a guaranteed return of a special new happiness.

I conducted a similar experiment when I took deeper notice of a lifelong friend, Jerald Kunz, who had been born blind. I wondered what Jerald felt each day, awakening from darkness into darkness. This was one of those days I felt a need to reevaluate my blessings and find a bit more happiness. I had again found myself falling victim to life's routine of unappreciation, and I decided on this Saturday morning I would be blind for a day.

Obtaining a large scarf as a blindfold, I started my new day without sight. I experienced at first the usual bumping into chairs in the living room and misjudging the positions of walls. But while I was thus inhibited, many things of life strangely came into focus. Eating without sight is barely imaginable! Judging distance and accuracy from table to mouth is only part of the problem. Whether or not something is on the fork when you start is an even greater concern. I took several trips to my mouth with an empty fork. I tried a spoon later, finding it somewhat easier. Fingers helped tremendously for loading the spoon. Television was shallow, the radio a blessing. Daily duties such as combing hair, putting on a tie straight (I tried it just for the experience), choosing the right colors of clothing, or "seeing" whether or not the shirt about to be put on was clean or not—all once simple tasks— were now sudden sources of frustration.

I was especially impressed out of doors. Driving was impossible. I just hung around the house. I felt the lawn and wished I could have enjoyed the color as well as the rich texture. A dog barked nearby. I tried to picture the kind of dog it was. Then I tried to imagine how I would visualize a dog of any kind, having never seen one before. I found the sense of touch of wonderful worth. I could not see the blue sky or the fluffy, beautiful cloud formations. A friend walked by and greeted me. I tried desperately to recognize the voice. It was difficult; it was frustrating. I thought of other complexities of problems not yet encountered in my self-imposed temporary blindness: the loveliness of a child's face, a young woman, my mother and father—not to know what their faces looked like; not to know what my own faced looked like!—a boat, a painting, my house. Oh, did this soul gain a great awakening and a new concept of vision. When the blindfold was removed, I was a reblessed person, renewed with appreciation for all my faculties. How vivid colors appeared. How warm my heart was. I felt almost a tinge of guilt, having so much. Try it sometime if you're down.

Learn to turn yourself on, rather than turn on yourself. Start to notice the little things in life. Some time ago a popular song ("Feelin' Groovy") stressed the need to "slow down, you move too fast, you got to make the morning last." It also mentioned taking note of the little, seemingly insignificant things in daily life—as in another line of the same song, "Hello lamppost, whatcha knowin'?" Who really cares what a lamppost knows? But you get the point.

Ever wonder why Disneyland is so appealing and enjoyable? It's the magnificent amount of detail in its creation. That's exactly what we should try to duplicate in daily life—to start becoming aware of life's many wonderful details, to awaken our senses to an appreciation of those things so often just taken for granted. I recall a poem entitled, I believe, "The World Is Mine," telling of a girl with only one foot, a blind boy, and a child who could not hear. "Oh, God, forgive me when I whine," the poet exclaims. "I'm blessed indeed! The world is mine!"

Quite another means that I personally find helpful to reappreciate my present circumstances and blessings is sometimes to recall past hardships, both my own and those of others, using the memory to trigger a new thankfulness for the lesser degree of the present problem or unhappiness. Usually, if you seek just a little, you can find a worse situation than the one you are presently experiencing. The comparison induces happiness. By the way, to add a more pleasant touch to the experience, you may try to make it a recall of a *humorous* bad situation.

As one personal example in my own life, when something is not just as I wish it would be I often allow my thoughts to wander back to old Denmark and the many months I spent on a bicycle, exposed to the elements. I vividly recollect that, compared with the present unhappiness, nothing could be as bad as one particular situation. It's a favorite bad memory of mine: it works every time in helping me find happiness. My companion, Elder Larsen, and I had to ride out for some distance to an evening appointment. It was in a blizzard. The snow and wind were beating down on us so heavily we were forced to dismount our bikes and push them. The wind was so great we had to lean almost horizontally against our bikes.

Suddenly my new J.C. Penney's hat went airborne and flew over a fence. It was a barbed wire fence, and I was forced to go through it carefully to retrieve my hat. Also, cows had been in the field prior to my arrival, necessitating that I watch my step. As I was going through the fence I heard a strange noise. I retrieved my hat, shook it off, and went back through the fence. Again I heard that funny, slicing noise. Returning to my bicycle and my waiting and very patient companion, I felt a bit of a draft about me. Looking down, I noticed the reason for the funny little noise each time I had passed through the fence. The barbed wire had caught the thin plastic raincoat I was wearing, neatly slicing it each time I went through the wire. I was discouraged, cold, and homesick. I was also now "blowing in the wind." We continued on our trek of another half mile or so through a little stretch of countryside between Odense and a neighboring village. The wind shifted to our left, and the sides of our faces took the bulk of the buffeting snow. My face was frozen, my ears worse. I reached up to my ears hoping to soothe them

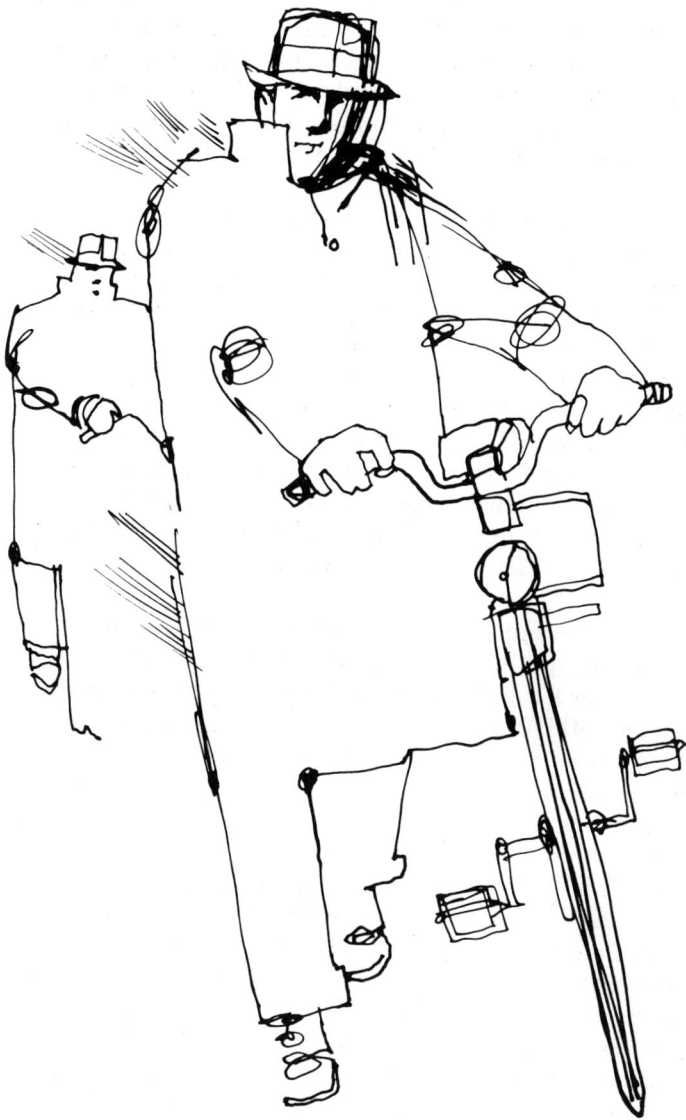

with any body warmth possible, and found, much to my surprise and added misery, snow packed tightly in my left ear. A tiny icicle hung from the ear lobe. I thought of home, my car (though old), and its wind-up windows, windshield, and top—all the luxury a person could want, not to mention the heater, radio, soft seats, and effortless ease of driving in almost any weather.

We finally arrived at our appointment, my thoughts, I must confess, focused much more on the warmth of their house than the message we had to bring. Though earlier in the day they had asked us with smiling faces to return this night, they now rejected us at the door when we arrived, and we remained in the cold. I could not believe this "atrocity" was knowingly perpetuated from one human being to another! Oh, I love my car—any car. Oh, I appreciate the weather—any weather seen from the window of my house or warm automobile. It's nice to learn the principle of appreciation. I makes one *happy*.

Another apt area of comparison for appreciating your own present situation is nourishment. Once a month at least, those faithful persons participating in the monthly fast feel the renewed appreciation for body-building and tasteful foods. When I was serving in the armed forces of our country, I recall during training being assigned, on one occasion, to guard a large, dual-wheeled, water tank trailer. We drove for miles in hills to station me at a lonely guard post. Arriving, I was let out, and with my trusty nine-pound M1 I stood guard next to this seemingly worthless empty water tank. The day was long, and I became hungry. Surrounding my post was a shield of forest. A dirt road aimlessly wound its way over the barren area where I stood, and shortly to the east disappeared into the thicket. During the long and slow afternoon I began feeling the lack of my accustomed noon meal. Apparently my sergeant had forgotten me.

Later in the day, I heard a distant, squeaky, rumbling noise in the forest. Focusing my eyes as well as I

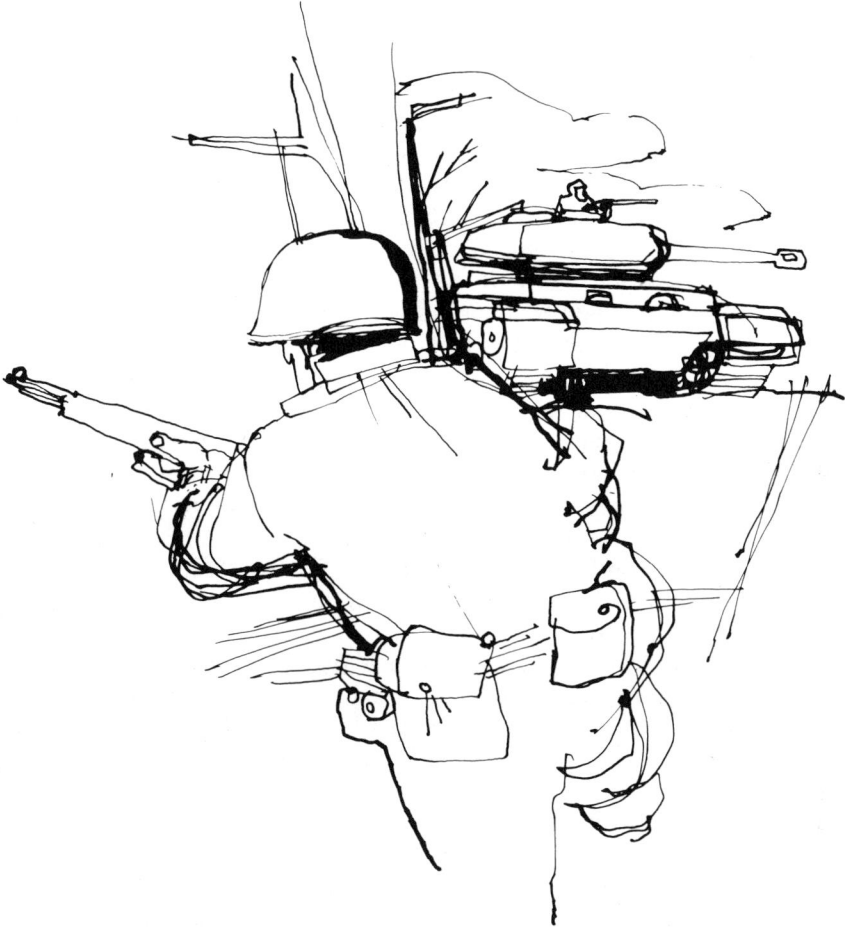

could into the dark of the massed trees, I saw what
appeared to be an approaching tank. It was a very
large, very impressive, and very oncoming "enemy"
tank! Hustling over to a nearby small cluster of trees,
I took immediate cover. Though only in mock battle
circumstances, I clutched my M1 rifle in firing position. Then I wondered, what good could it do against
a tank? The tank soon stopped at just about the same
place I had previously been standing. The upper hatch
opened, and from its impressive height a man peered

out. He carefully scanned the area, saw nothing, dropped down the heavy, steel door, and again was on his way.

There seems to be nothing to compare with the sound of this type of military vehicle. With its unusual squeaky, clattering sound, it lends a chill of fear. I feared. I allowed the situation to be "real." Many thoughts very quickly flashed through my mind when that mechanical monster came upon me. Hunger was not one of the thoughts; life was: appreciation for being alive; a sudden overview of the too often unseen or unappreciated blessings which make life what it can be—simple but meaningful blessings: taking early advantage of daily opportunities rather than getting another coveted hour of sleep, thus missing a beautiful sunrise and that early morning chilly freshness, or the opportunity to get something special accomplished, or whatever.

As the tank clattered away into the forest, I quickly reviewed, as if my life had actually been in jeopardy, the many things I would do from that day forward to enjoy and appreciate my life more fully. That momentary, seemingly insignificant, chapter in a soldier's life has caused me many times to reevaluate my life at a moment's glance and make certain of continual appreciation of the little things.

Late that evening I heard another rumble coming up the road, and again I found myself reenacting the previous scene. This time, however, the vehicle that stopped at about the same place was a large supply truck, and a voice called out, "Black!" I yelled back to advance and be recognized, which the man did, identifying himself as my sergeant, with a few additional words to the affect that "someone apparently forgot you out here." I hastily agreed, and he threw a small ration can to me and departed. My miniature can opener, which hung on my dog tag chain, was immediately put to work. It was time to eat! Peering into the opened can, I saw white, thick grease. I was familiar with the contents. This was a can containing highly nutritious packed hamburger patties, and the

16

heavy white stuff would have been a tasty gravy had the can been heated. But it wasn't! I took out my bayonet and carefully scooped and scraped the gravy away and onto the ground. It was inedibly cold, but I was hungry! With a jabbing action, I caught one patty at a time and feasted. It was good—vaguely sickening, but good. How I appreciate every meal now. Often I hear my wife make excuse for not preparing a more appealing meal. I simply reply, "It's great honey!" And it is. As a reminder of those days, I keep a small fragment of a hand grenade I tossed during that time of my life, along with my mini can opener.

Maybe some of you remember the patriotic songs sung stateside during the great and terrible World War II. One such song was entitled, "Say a Prayer for the Boys Over There!" Remember it? My older brother and I used to sing it when we were little tykes. I recall the tears in the eyes of the older folks whenever we would perform it. I wondered why. Now, whenever there arises a political skirmish, police action, or whatever they call it when another nation and ourselves are shooting live bullets at each other, I allow this inspired song to come to mind. Maybe it is because of my own time of crawling under flying bullets and bomb bursts. Maybe it brings to mind the agony, hate, and blood of war. Maybe, too, I know in my heart that somewhere in the world, on a battle-ground, there is a guy over there, needing prayer, sitting in a foxhole, no longer thinking of the luxury of a meal, but rather thinking about his few remaining rounds of ammo, hoping in some miraculous way our guys can get a chopper through enemy fire to drop not a food supply, but deadly, life-giving rounds of ammunition. I thought of these things this Thanksgiving, uttering a silent thanks to those guys out there, and making myself take time out to appreciate my own blessed present standard of living and the abundance and variety of foods placed before me. This especially came to mind when I was helping myself to seconds, smelling the aroma of freshly baked pies from out in the kitchen. The whole idea

17

embraces the principle of being grateful and appreciative for what you have, using a possible negative situation as a reminder if necessary, a concept Paul refers to in 2 Corinthians 12:7, when he mentions his "thorn in the flesh." "For when I am weak," he says, "then am I strong" (verse 10).

Here is a collection of additional tiny tips to help renew appreciation, and, hopefully, happiness:

1. Occasionally, gather up and put away little treasured things about the house or your bedroom. In six months or so bring them out again. It's surprising how nice they look after you have not seen them for a while. If married, put them in your cedar chest, and the two of you open it together. A tiny feeling like the magic of Christmas fills the air. Talk about an easy way to gain renewed appreciation for little things of life once taken for granted. This works.

2. Next time on the freeway or open highway, clipping along at sixty or seventy miles per hour, take a few moments out to give a thought about our pioneer forefathers earlier in history, covering the same ground at five to ten miles *per day*, with wheels often bogging down, having to dig them out by hand—not to mention sickness along the way and delivery of babies in a covered wagon in nearly intolerable sub-zero weather or blistering desert heat. Remember the six thousand souls buried out there.

3. Think of some masterfully written song lyrics. I am reminded of two in particular, which go something like this: "When you're weary and you can't sleep, count your blessings instead of sheep, and you'll go to sleep counting your blessings"; and "The world belongs to everyone, the best things in life are free." One version of this latter song outlines in detail the many "free" things in life: the stars, the changing sky, the clouds, the rain, the wind, the sun, the mountains, the streams, the trees, and last but not least, the

18

beautiful and fascinating animal kingdom—a great resource of added happiness.

4. Next time you use the phone, appreciate not having to change your clothes, bundle up, pretty up, and go out in possible stormy weather to carry the same message you can transmit in a few moments through the touch of your finger, from the convenience of your warm, comfortable home.

5. Make whatever you are worthwhile! Do your best. Gain the satisfaction of doing a good job and being proud of your accomplishments and yourself. If you park cars for a living, don't be just a car parker. Be an Automotive Placement Engineer! Put some class and confidence into your life. Be the best of whatever you are. Strive continually to do better. This little poem by Douglas Malloch emphasizes the point well:

If you can't be a pine on the top of the hill,
  Be a scrub in the valley—but be
The best little scrub by the side of the rill;
  Be a bush if you can't be a tree.

If you can't be a bush be a bit of the grass,
  And some highway happier make;
If you can't be a muskie then just be a bass—
  But the liveliest bass in the lake!

We can't all be captains, we've got to be crew,
  There's something for all of us here,
There's big work to do, and there's lesser to do,
  And the task you must do is the near.

If you can't be a highway then just be a trail,
  If you can't be the sun be a star;
It isn't by size that you win or you fail—
  *Be the best of whatever you are!**

*"Be the Best of Whatever You Are," courtesy of Bell-McClure Syndicate.

6. Again, appreciate what you have. You could have less. When I was a little boy we couldn't afford to have real working "walkie-talkies"—you know, the kind you see in the war movies when men are talking to each other through those funny rectangular boxes with aerials sticking out on top. We did with what we had. The tin cans with tightly stretched string were all right, but wouldn't work around corners very successfully; so we soon discovered that an old garden hose could be heard much better when spoken into, even around corners! When we got tired of talking "war" through the hose, the device provided another means of producing added fun and frolic. There was always just enough water left in the hose that with a great enough effort one could blow it into the awaiting listening ear at the other end, starting a "real" war with water, adding to the fun. We had more fun with this trick than any real, expensive walkie-talkie ever could have produced.

The whole idea is summed up in the fact that much potential happiness lies dormant all around us in every facet of our lives. But motivation is needed to use it; it takes some doing, and even some creativity. It is hoped that these suggestions will help, or at least spur your own imagination in the same direction, that you will get more ideas of your own. So with all thy getting, go!

Now a word about another kind of changeable imperfection. It was Abe Lincoln who said something to the effect, "Always tell the truth and you won't have to remember what you have said." He was referring to the principle of personal integrity or honesty, both while in the spotlight and silently, while alone. Here is a sleeper for potential, warm inner happiness many folks overlook. Every day people of all walks of life lose out in this area of happiness when they, in greater or lesser degree, cheat their neighbor, grocer, employer, merchant and so forth.

Elder Hartman Rector, Jr., put it this way: "Ever walk by a pay phone or other vending machine and innocently drop your finger into the coin return slot? What were you looking for?" Good question, isn't it? Maybe you have heard about Elder Sterling W. Sill's little experience at the service station and the soft drink machine. Thirsty, he put a coin into the machine and made his choice of drink. Taking the bottle from the machine, he noticed his coin returned. He picked it up and suddenly found himself in a very interesting, though challenging, situation. For a few moments part of the other side of man came out in him. Desiring to return the dime, he quickly thought if he put the coin back into the machine another drink would come out—and possibly the coin again. People being as they are, another thought quickly jumped into his mind: "I'll keep the dime. They charge too much for these things anyway!" Immediately this thought was superseded by a compounding thought of the dishonesty in this action, and then he seriously pondered his sudden dilemma. He said to himself, "What would you do if you had put the coin into the machine and *nothing* came out? Yes, that's right. You'd be over to the station attendant in no time at all." And that's what Brother Sill did. Returning the coin to the rightful owner, he walked away from this interesting little incident in life, a greater and happier person in a small but so significant way.

I was enjoying Walt Disney's Magic Kingdom, Disneyland, on one of those days you wonder if you should be there at all. The crowds were enormous. We stood in line for the usual forty-five-minute wait for the famed Matterhorn ride, and our turn finally arrived. With so many people rushing the ticket taker, I found myself being innocently shoved through the portal, arriving on the loading side of the attraction with my ticket still in hand, and no one but me aware of the difference. That same series of thoughts Brother Sill had had raced through my mind. They would never know the difference with all these

21

people paying, and besides, I had been a faithful customer of the "Kingdom" for many years. This would be a little remuneration for my faithfulness. And quite another thing—this ticket would also serve for the Pirates of the Caribbean on the other side of the park, and I liked the Pirates of the Caribbean!

Oh, what a lot of rationalization. But it was all there, and for the moment I thought myself justified. Then I caught hold and seriously reviewed my sudden situation. Catching the "trick" of it all, I turned around into the oncoming line of people and slowly made my way back toward the clean-cut young man

taking tickets. I soon got the sign from him and others in line, however, that my action was not lending itself to the greatest ease for the system. By the time I got to the ticket taker there were many wondering what I could possibly want by this strange reversed action. The young fellow immediately asked what the problem was; I told him he neglected to take my ticket, and I handed it to him.

He looked at me somewhat puzzled, wondering if I was OK, realizing, I suppose, what many would have done in a similar situation. He smiled and thanked me. His thanks was a very special one, a thanks that had a special heart and soul warmer with it.

It's almost humorous how those innocently involved with surprise honesty sometimes react in this type of situation. Once while at dinner with my wife and her parents, we ordered our meals and shortly after received our salads. Following the meal we prepared to leave. Obtaining the check, I noticed that the young lady had neglected adding the extra cost of the salads. For the moment I said nothing, hoping for a little possible fun. Then, handing the check to the cashier, I said in a solemn tone, "There is an error on our check."

She looked it over carefully and then quickly, almost defiantly, reported, I don't think so, sir." It was amusing how quickly her defense mechanism went into effect.

I then with a slight smile informed her that the establishment was cheating itself of the cost of four salads. It took a few moments for her to recognize a good deed was happening. It seemed to be so unrelated to the usual.

Thinking this matter over later, I thought of the many little incidents like this in life, which, if only given a little more concern, could serve as excellent sources of additional happiness. These kinds of experiences bring on their own sort of inner happiness, unparalleled by other happiness producers. It's refreshing to be on top of little favorite, common temptations, and to be master of self—doing thirty in a thirty-miles-per-hour zone, for instance, or seventy in a seventy-miles-per-hour zone.

I once had the opportunity of visiting the home of a friend, Dale Tingey, then the Assistant Administrator of Church Seminaries and Institutes. I was on an extended visit from California, on seminary business, and was invited to stay at his lovely home in Provo. Both having business in Salt Lake City the

following day, we arose early in the morning. Brother
Tingey was driving, and it was at the time when much
freeway construction was under way between Provo
and Salt Lake City. As the hour was very early, we
clipped along without incident.

We approached a construction zone, but there was
no obstruction of any kind—just a large sign that
read, "Construction Zone Next Three Miles. Slow to
35." We had been doing an honest sixty-five miles an
hour. It was too early for workmen to be on the job,
and we were still far out in a rural area. There was no
apparent reason in my mind for reducing our speed. I
noticed, though, as we passed the large sign that
Brother Tingey let his foot off the gas pedal, and we
drove those three miles at thirty-five miles an hour. I
marvelled, but then took another long look at the
situation. So much more was really going on than I
had realized. Not only was he abiding by a law, no
matter how small or insignificant it seemed, but
another little incident was silently taking place that
day way out on a seemingly insignificant section of
the freeway. Brother Tingey, all by himself, was
exercising personal integrity. He did not feel the
difference between seventy and thirty-five miles per
hour worth the compromise of his standards. Oh,
how I learned that day.

Funny about the worth of integrity in the minds of
individuals. In the aerospace industry there was a great
problem with employees stealing. Great emphasis was
placed upon personal integrity, and they sponsored
all types of honesty programs to help alleviate the
problem. One point emphatically brought to mind
was the different values placed upon personal integrity. Some sold their integrity for a nickel pencil. One
man thought more of his integrity, however. He
wrapped a twenty-five-dollar bandsaw blade around
his waist, but upon customarily showing his lunch
bucket to the security officer at the gate after work,
accidently released the pressure from his arms holding
the saw blade securely to his waist. Before the eyes of
the surprised guard, it unravelled and fell to the

24

ground. He not only lost his job, but think of the self-induced unhappiness that man experienced, especially upon having to report to his family the reason he lost his job. A twenty-five-dollar bandsaw blade!

I've often thought, while in school, how much better it is to *earn* your possible lower grade than to be haunted the rest of your life with an *unearned*, dishonest higher mark, especially when you realize how distant in memory grades become as the years go by—that is, the honest grades. The dishonest ones linger, a constant tell-tale secret, forever plaguing the mind. Yes, here is a great source of potential inner happiness and warmth: personal integrity. Include it in your program for acquiring greater happiness in your life.

Now, last but not least, we must consider one other important factor: the real, personal troubles and problems found in daily life, causing much unhappiness. They exist and can't be denied. But happiness can even be squeezed out of personal unhappiness. Sometimes the results are realized later, but somehow they generally come forth.

For example—on a lighter vein for a moment—if you have a canker sore in your mouth, and you bite into a big, juicy orange, or grab a handful of potato chips, that's far from happiness, isn't it? But how about when that terrible thing is gone? We wouldn't even realize the difference between bad and good if we could not experience both. There would be no comparison of unhappiness and happiness. Now, if you don't have a canker sore in your mouth, bite into an orange and be appreciative. Go ahead, take a handful of those potato chips and munch on them. Enjoy the painless, delightful experience.

The same idea can apply to sickness. Don't you suddenly appreciate your daily, usually ignored, good health when you are down with the flu? Our lives are so busy that the only time we allot ourselves to appreciate our good health is when we are forced to take time out to get well! Strange, isn't it, how appreciation and even happiness can come from a small thing such as a canker sore or the flu? Everything really has its place in life, doesn't it? Even troubles and problems—serious ones too. In a strange way, serious dilemmas all seem eventually to find their place for good in our total development and experiences in life, and somehow to add a unique dimension to our happiness.

Now in finalizing this little trend of thought, remember the old saying, "If everyone's troubles were thrown in a pile together, and you were given the chance to choose from any of those assembled, chances are good that you would take your own troubles back again."

Acceptance of self, improvement where possible, confidence, sensitivity to life's little offerings, appreciation, and the strange principle of gratitude in adversity all together produce a giant and important segment of the total happiness of man. Now to the second key to happiness.

Second Key

*Maintain good physical
and spiritual health.*

Maintain good physical and spiritual health. This key includes several simple principles. First, get enough sleep—not too much, but enough to feel good, to rise in the morning rested and invigorated. To determine how many hours of sleep you need, a little experimentation might be necessary. Some people require very few hours of rest to feel fine all day, while others require a full eight to ten. You make this decision, but in doing so, be honest with yourself.

I recall Elder Marion G. Romney during a conference address saying, more or less off the cuff, something to the effect that he was grateful to his sweet companion for letting him sleep *late* this particular morning—till 5:30! Elder Thomas S. Monson once mentioned desiring, in his early days of apostleship, to come down to the office early in the morning in order to arrive earlier than President McKay, a man who, as you might recall, maintained that a man's most productive and most undisturbed time of the day is the very early hours of the morning. Elder Monson wanted to beat the president to the job. As the story goes, he came one morning at 6:00 and noticed the light of President McKay's office already on. The following morning he arrived at 5:30, but still behind the president. The next day he arrived about 5:00 a.m., but still was greeted by the already burning light of the prophet.

Maybe these great men are trying to tell us something. This little early morning secret might just be a key to longevity, productivity, and good health: enough sleep, but not too much. It seems like old-fashioned wisdom doesn't it? It is. President Brigham Young maintained the same principle of scheduled rest during the grand exodus of Saints across the plains to the Salt Lake Valley.

But beyond all these wise admonitions, the Lord has said it most clearly to Joseph in section 88, verse 124 of the Doctrine and Covenants: "Cease to sleep longer than is needful; retire to thy bed early, that ye

29

may not be weary; arise early, that your bodies and your minds may be invigorated."

Second, eat good, wholesome food. A cola and candy bar are not good food! Take time out to reward the body for doing such a good job every day. We treat our automobiles this way, with correct gasoline, the best oil, and miscellaneous additives, all to help them do a good, safe, dependable job. Give the body the same royal treatment and notice the improved running condition.

Third, maintain good personal hygiene. This means taking a good bath or shower regularly. To our young folks, it's turning on the water and then getting in! Use soap.

When finished, plan another type of cleansing. We call it repentance. Take a little inventory. Remove from your life any cobwebs collected during the week. Clean the dusty shelves. When I owned a little retail business some years ago, it was necessary to take inventory regularly. This procedure required getting rid of the bad stuff which didn't sell, and replacing it with good products. Dusting shelves was a regular daily activity. So it is with life. We need a regular inventory. Use another type of soap, in another sort of bathing—the soap called repentance and a rinsing called forgiveness. It's all in the plan, and is referred to as physical and spiritual personal hygiene. It's good for a fresh, new start in life, whenever you feel the need for it. When cleansing spiritually, kneel down and have a nice talk with your Heavenly Father.

Fourth, include occasional exercise in your daily schedule. Most folks don't have a lot of spare time for this but we should *take* time. Remember, even a little exercise is better than none. Here are a few tips:

1. When there is a choice between stairs and an elevator take the stairs.
2. When going somewhere on foot, jog or run a little on the way.
3. Instead of driving to the store, walk.

4. Swim occasionally.
5. Try a little tennis, handball, basketball, or ping pong. Get that blood circulating.
6. Drink lots of water. Water is one of life's miracles, you know.
7. Buy or borrow a bicycle, and enjoy a short ride in the evenings.

Any of the above, plus others you might think of, will make you feel just a little better each day. And when your body feels better, you also feel happier. Now put all the steps together, and welcome a little more happiness into your life. How are you doing?

Third Key

Cultivate a good sense of humor.

Cultivate a good sense of humor. This starts, strangely enough, with the ability to laugh at yourself. "Hey, Birdlegs!" Laugh it off.

It also requires being able to laugh with others. "Hey, Birdlegs!" Laugh it off with them. It's just being able to laugh!

Prerequisite to this ability is an appreciation for humor, usually called a sense of humor. It takes effort sometimes to develop a good sense of humor. Some think it comes from pseudo-intellectual girly magazines. These humor seekers are trapped on a one-way, dead-end street, facing a No-U-Turn sign, experiencing monthly a form of rationalization we call lying to yourself. I've heard the supposedly sincere argument that you don't have to look at the pictures. That's correct; you don't. But show me the man who faithfully follows such a publication and is able to pass over Miss Whoever-She-Is, found in the easy-to-open center section, in living color. King David couldn't. Rome couldn't. The odds are great in our sex-saturated society that the average man can't either. Why try to fight the odds? Granted, the so-called dirty jokes are some of the most skillful, but isn't this one of Satan's six-thousand-year-old tricks—being clever, and closely paralleling the real thing with a plastic counterfeit? Good humor and the appreciation of it are found in the spirit, not in the mire.

I remember one particular day on the job while I was associated with the aerospace industry. The "thing" of the day was to congregate near the coffee machine and listen to the department's joke teller relate his latest. Most were in bad taste. I was young, and inexperienced in the big, new world of industry versus young testimony. Prior to this day, I had attempted to ride out the circumstances gracefully, knowing full well my guilt, but not being able to muster enough of that badly needed commodity called courage of conviction. Listening when I knew inside it was wrong haunted my mind for many weeks, as the feeling of guilt was immediately awakened whenever the uncomfortable joke time arose. But somehow I would find myself in the midst of those involved. They were my friends.

Well, this day, our court jester proceeded to tell us the "best one yet." Gathering slowly, but surely, all the courage I could, I decided this would be the day I would react somehow the way an active Christian should. I wasn't certain myself what that reaction would be. As the joke began to be told, I quietly interrupted and asked if this was one of the usual type—specifically, was it "dirty or not?" A quick response from the man in charge confirmed my suspicions. With all the strength just worked for, I quickly made the decision and replied emphatically, "See you later!" Then I walked away, down the hallway.

The men stood there, looking somewhat stunned, but at last one called, "What's the matter with you?" Then I heard the traditional calling of "funny" names, but one remark was heard loud and clear above the rest: "Hey, look, everybody! There goes Snow White!"

This hurt. At first I had a typical boyish desire to "get even." But with quick afterthought, I discovered the comment actually to be a compliment in many ways. I thought of the young lady, Snow White, her character, her love, and reputation throughout the world. I thought too of her seven neat little friends. Gosh, I thought, that isn't bad at all. Then Walt Disney's wonderful Magic Kingdom came to mind— Main Street, Pirates of the Caribbean, the Matterhorn Bobsled Ride, and other warm, gala settings. Suddenly I liked what they chose to call me. In fact, I felt an unusual pride about it. I smiled, said a polite "Thank you," and walked on down the hall. When I returned to my desk some moments later and approached my friends, I felt assured of further needling; so I mustered up a little more courage and entered the work area whistling the popular tune of the Seven Dwarfs, "Heigh-ho, heigh-ho, it's off to work we go!" They laughed; then I laughed. I had won a very important private war. I had a warm feeling of personal victory I had never quite experienced before. It was a clean, good, comforting feeling, deep in my spirit—a feeling even encompassing respect.

Let humor become an added little blessing in your life. Although counterfeited by Satan, it's sent from God. Learn the difference.

By the way, the following day "the boys" again met at the coffee machine to hear the latest joke. From force of habit I had joined my friends, when the joke teller looked over at me and politely said, "I don't think you'd want to hear this one, Don." I thanked him, excused myself, and met them back at our work area.

Fourth Key

Be a friend.

Be a Friend. "Do unto others . . ." Sounds simple enough doesn't it? Have you ever stopped to realize, though, how many people don't even know their own neighbors? It's quite a common thing, especially in the larger cities. They often live next door for several years, yet have never called a greeting of any sort across the fence. Being a friend, like other keys to happiness, brings with it its own peculiar reward. A definite, unique, good feeling comes over you when you befriend someone, or do good to others, especially when you do such good deeds and remain anonymous.

Some young folks know the need to be befriended. Schools are full of the problem. Those involved can be called the "no-name" kids—the kids who come faithfully to school each day, silently "do their thing," and go home again, scarcely noticed by anyone. They might be the ones who didn't attempt to become cheerleaders or athletes, who didn't try out for the debate team, the choir, or a special committee of one sort or another. The reason? They lack confidence, they have no friends to encourage them, they are not popular, and so on.

What would happen if you singled out one of these people? It doesn't have to be in a hallway at school. It can be at work, in the neighborhood, at church, at the club—just about anywhere. Single such a person out; strike up a conversation; find out a little about him. Acknowledge his existence.

Another interesting approach is to sit down and write that person a little note. It might simply read, "I know something good about you!" or, "I think you're swell!" or, "I like you!" Then sign it with a couple of question marks, drop it in an envelope, seal it, address it, and send it. To measure the amount of good such a simple task could do for such a person would probably be impossible. It could be one of the most valuable therapies imaginable. Give it a try.

My brother Richard always practiced the concept, even at the peril of his own reputation and, in some cases, personal safety. Once he and a couple of friends were on a hunting party when they came upon a group of people standing beside the dirt logging road on which they were traveling. The people appeared to be concerned about something, and upon closer observation the reason for their concern became apparent. Stopping their truck, my brother and his friends got out and asked one of the onlookers what had happened.

A man looked up, and pointing down the canyon said, "Been a terrible accident. Two men in a jeep. That one over there is probably dead. The other at the bottom of the canyon near the jeep we don't know about." Sleeping bags, guns, and camping equipment lay strewn down the canyon.

"What's being done to help?" Richard asked.

The man replied something to this effect: "What can a guy do with them 'way down in that canyon?"

Richard and his friends had just returned from active duty in the Korean conflict; they knew what

could be done. They started organizing that scene like a combat-ready mission. The man who had done the speaking had a truck with a large cable hoist on the front bumper. Richard yelled an order to him to get into his truck and move it close to the edge of the cliff. Another was sent to the forestry service for help. Another directed traffic, keeping the area clear for any necessary action. Securing the line from the hoist around his waist, Richard started his way down the precarious cliff, the man in the truck letting him down the steep incline carefully, foot by foot. He edged his way over to the first man, but the man was dead. Quickly changing his course he started the descent to the bottom and to the other man. As he approached, he could hear the man groaning. The jeep lay partially on the man's leg.

Richard signaled for help, and others began the descent down the cable to the scene. Together, the men worked the jeep off the injured man's leg, and carefully began carrying him up the painstakingly long ascent back to the highway above. The going was slow; the man was heavy. But what was in the hearts of those men? Very possibly sentiments reflecting the lyrics of a recent song, "He ain't heavy, he's my brother." Because of their involvement, the man lives today. There is no way to describe the kind of happiness that comes from serving others.

Now, granted, the majority of us don't have this kind of situation in our lives, but the principle applies to everyday life as well. What about the little widow woman down the street? She may need her lawn mowed, or some leaves raked. How about a loaf of homebaked bread? *Everyone* likes homebaked bread. A dozen cookies? A pie? A friendly visit? A ride downtown? Some painting or repair? The possibilities are almost limitless. People are not accustomed to such goodness. I tell my teen-age friends when they walk down the street to really surprise an elderly man or woman walking toward them, with a great big, friendly, "Hello there!" After the initial shock, the older person will be very pleased that a "real" teen-

43

ager spoke *kind* words to him. A great deal of his information about teen-agers has been negative—drug abuse, crime, stories that sell newspapers. From a simple, friendly hello his hope for the youth of this great nation will increase considerably.

Begin to notice others in life. My brother taught me this principle years ago when we were high school boys. He was very popular in high school. It seemed everyone liked him: the hoods, the popular students, the sportsmen, the no-names. I recall an incident I shall never forget, which reflected his way of helping others. I was standing in the hallway one day, talking with a couple of my friends. I had just entered high school and in a way sailed right in on big brother's good reputation. I hadn't learned yet that good reputations come through continual, conscientious effort. We noticed my brother walking down the corridor with one of the very unknown, very unpopular girls of the school. She was at least a hundred pounds overweight and hadn't quite learned about personal hygiene or appearance, and most kids in the school didn't care much for her. But here before our eyes walked one of the most popular guys in school with one of the most unpopular girls. That was something. As he passed by us, I sarcastically whispered, "Not doing so good these days, huh, brother?"

He looked up, and with stern expression on his face said, "Talk to you in a moment." He then continued down the hallway with that girl before the eyes of the entire student body. I noticed others giving him the same look as we. He was walking with her and carrying on a regular, normal conversation. When they arrived at the far end of the hallway leading to another wing of the building, he opened the door for her, in front of all those people! They continued down the hall and to her class, and there he stood and talked to her until the tardy bell rang. Bidding her good-bye, he turned and started his trek back to where we were standing; but his pace was unlike that of his first passing. We had begun to

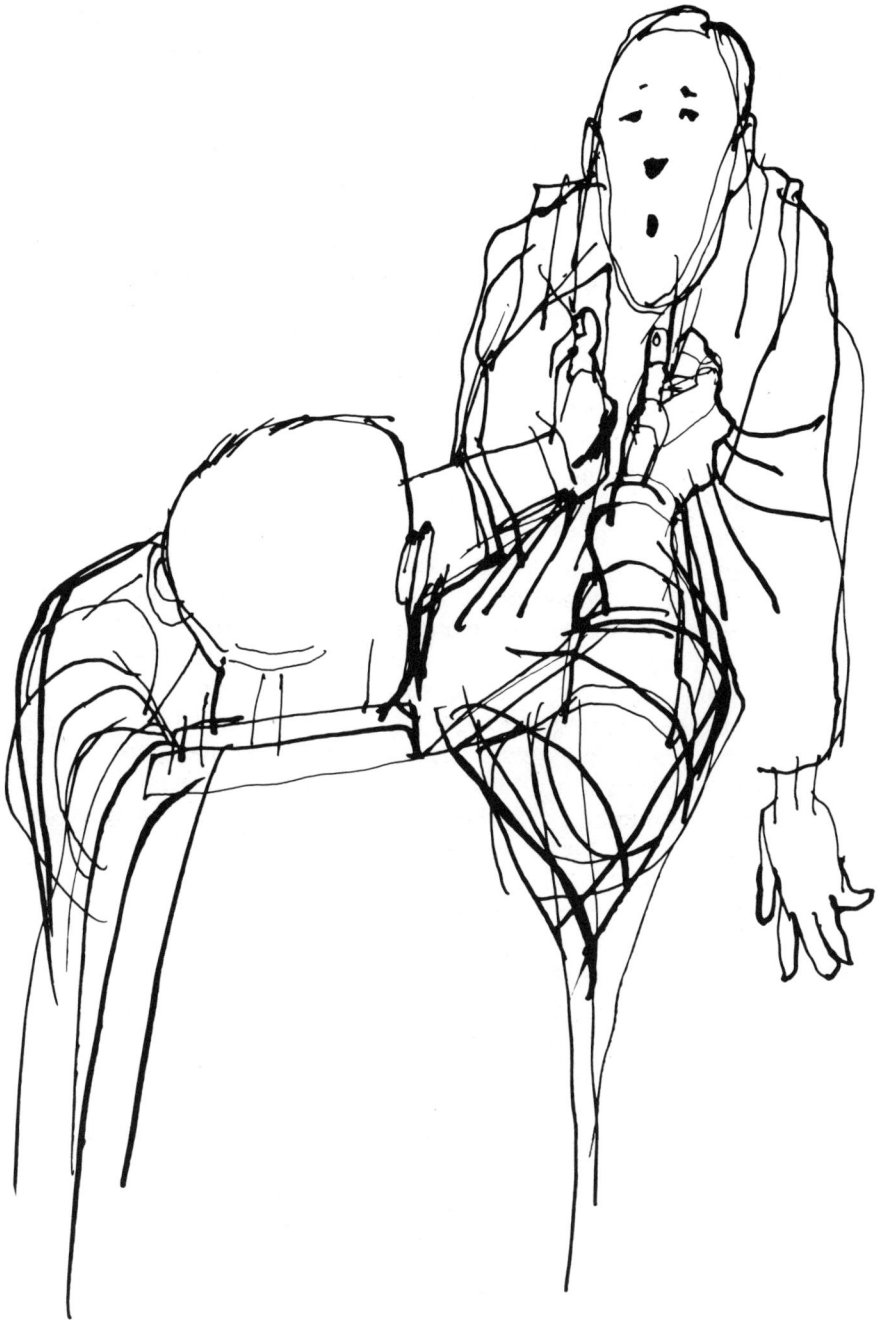

disperse when we heard a voice, loud and clear, resonate from down the hallway: "Hold it right there, you guys!" We held it right there. He was not only a much bigger fellow than we, but when a voice has that kind of command in it, you stay.

Very shortly he arrived, and in one great motion walked almost right into me, grabbed me by the front of the shirt with clenched fists, and hoisted me right up the wall, before the eyes of my buddies and the passersby. It was the first time I had looked down on my brother. I was embarrassed.

Then he began one of the most penetrating oral thrashings I had ever experienced. Oh, it was a time of real learning, together with exposure to the great big world of growing up. To the best of my recollection, he said, "I heard what you said when I passed by you. Maybe she did too, I don't know. But I want to tell you something that I never want you to forget." Then he used a word popular at the time, "Do you *dig* me?" With continual movement of his right pointing finger, he repeated the question, simultaneously poking his finger into my skinny chest. It hurt each time he did it, and the repeated question whether or not I "dug" him was quickly answered. I did! I dug him. Oh, did I. My buddies started to leave, but he quickly reminded them they had "better stay for a while!" He then continued his on-the-spot dissertation. He said, "I know full well what you were thinking when we passed you. Chances are excellent you don't know that girl. I want to teach you a lesson about people. Don't you ever think that you are *that* great that you can choose your friends by outward appearance only. There is a school full of no-name kids walking these halls each day who are sterling in character and goodness. Slow down and start taking time to notice people inside, instead of this society's crummy attitude of outside only. Whether they are fat, skinny, tall or short, you start checking the spirits of people and you'll have a great, new experience coming to you. Dig?"

I dug. I was also still up in the air, against the wall.

46

I felt a loss of youthful pride, but in a strange way I also felt very humble. Everything he said had a deep ring of truth in it. I had been caught in society's rut. He closed off his impromptu lecture by reminding me that one must *work* for a good reputation, and that if I didn't start immediately on mine I would soon lose what little I had. That day in the hallway of our high school, Richard got through to his little and inexperienced brother.

I awakened to a new world, a world of noticing and helping others, and I started to apply this new philosophy in my own young life. The following day or so at school, still haunted by my brother's "thrashing," I began taking note of the many no-name kids in the hallways. Looking a bit closer, I found them to be people, just like the "name" kids, but not quite as much in the limelight. I singled out such a girl in my civics class, whom I sat next to. I sat there for many moments accumulating as much courage as possible, to try my new-found philosophy, so emphatically taught me by my brother. I was ready. With all the courage now mustered up, I turned, and with great hesitation said, "Hi!"

A new dawn broke. This "nobody" came alive. With surprising sweetness and warmth, she replied, "Hello."

A conversation ensued, one of which opened my inexperienced eyes even wider. I learned that she wasn't the "brain" everyone said she was, that at night, after school, she studied very diligently and worked hard for her good grades. Her musical talent, which everyone took for granted, likewise demanded long, hard hours of practicing. I began to appreciate my find. What an interesting, nice person she was. I also felt ashamed of my past false impressions and verbal opinions. Suddenly I had a new friend, and I really liked her. Our friendship grew until we both looked forward to seeing each other each day. What a joyful experience it was, and how grateful I am that it happened. For that small episode in a young boy's life opened new horizons for future, and now highly cherished, friendships with all types of people.

Years passed, and the opportunity of being a friend and doing good to others became a normal, daily part of life's experiences. I recall such an experience, which took place one summer while I was living in southern California. It was a beautiful, warm, sunny Saturday morning. The neighborhood was slowly awakening to the sound of lawnmowers clattering in the distance. We were renting an old, white, framed, two-story house. I was passing an open upstairs window when I suddenly became aware of the strangest sound coming from the street below. Looking out, I saw two men standing over a third, who was lying prostrate, facedown on the pavement. The strange noise was the result of a violent epileptic seizure. He was raising himself up with his arms and cruelly thrusting his face down onto the hard pavement. The strange sound was the sound of breaking bone and flesh. The two men watched with their hands in their pockets.

The effect of my early training session of befriending and helping others was automatically activated in my mind. I immediately called to my wife to telephone the police and to have them send for an ambulance, while I grabbed a towel and ran downstairs to the street below. Now I had studied the effects of epilepsy, but had never actually been involved with a case. I recognized this as a grand mal seizure, and I knew that the victim was unaware of his self-inflicted injuries and danger. As I approached, thoughts flashed through my mind: the thought of the good Samaritan, compounded with another thought of a possible lawsuit for helping. That seemed to be popular these days. But there was another feeling even stronger and more important than the fear of being sued. That was my concern for a fellow human being, one of my brothers, who needed help—*now.*

I looked, puzzled, at the others standing there, and then straddled the downed man on my knees, and during one of his upward motions, quickly placed the folded towel in the area of impact. He again came down as before; however, this time his face hit the soft, clean towel. I felt inspired that very moment to place my chest next to his back, maybe for a sacred exchange of human warmth and spirit. I placed one hand under his face, and put my head close to his, and calmly said to him, "You're going to be all right. We have help coming for you." I repeated the communication several times, and his convulsive movements began to slow down. Then his eyes began to focus, and his breathing took on a more normal rate. Finally, slowly, he stopped the action completely, laid his head softly on my folded towel, and lay there quietly. I continued to comfort him with the closeness of my own body, at the same time talking to him quietly.

By this time there was the excitement of oncoming sirens, a gathering crowd, and police appearing on the scene. Ambulance attendants made their way through the onlookers. The man's eyes looked deeply into mine. He said nothing. He couldn't. But his spirit told me of his gratitude. As they placed him on the stretcher and rushed him away, I slowly made my way through the crowd and walked across the street to my home. Again in my life I had had the privilege to feel that good, warm, satisfying feeling of having given to another—even one of our Heavenly Father's own children in need. Oh, it is a good feeling. It is happiness sublime.

A few other examples: One day my wife called me at work and reminded me to pick up a few things at the store, including chocolate, sugar, butter, and nuts—the ingredients of good, old-fashioned, home-made fudge. I was pleased. Upon arriving home, however, I was told the fudge was to be made and given to families and friends around the neighborhood as little Christmas tokens. I was selfishly a little disappointed. The fudge was made and packaged in separate tinfoil containers, and we started out on our "giving mission." We delivered the gifts to most of the families without their knowledge, just leaving them on porches, and departing. As we visited each house, a warmer and warmer feeling came over me. I was again feeling that spark of special happiness from giving to others. This anyone can do. Try it.

A young family moved into our town as recent converts to the Church. Previously, they had been followers of the "hippie" subculture, but now, as converts to the real truth, desiring to be closer to the brethren and the center of the Church activities, they decided to move to Utah. They left their California residence with about ninety-five percent faith and five extra dollars. They even had need to "bless" their car coming across the desert, as it literally came to a halt with the old engine smoking and billowing. They made it to Utah!

It was the Christmas season, the time of giving. They needed, and we were aware of it. Together with some seminary students, we decided how nice it would be to do something for that family. We felt that a box of fresh fruit would be appreciated; so off to the market we went. As we began putting various fruits into the basket, the spirit of the occasion grew. Oranges, apples, bananas, raisins, a fresh pineapple, a coconut, plus cranberries for added color filled the box. Fresh mixed nuts in the shell were added.

But the spirit had not finished inspiring. Karen, one of the girls present, grabbed some vegetables, Jill some bread and butter. Then with some additional final items, we topped the adventure with a large frozen turkey. We were actually laughing with special happiness as we pushed that cart down the aisle. We went home, prepared the whole gift in an open box wrapped with Christmas paper, and attached a disguised little note to the effect, "We love you all. Merry Christmas."

Delivery was made later that night. We placed the box at the front door, banged on the door, and ran to the waiting car in the street. The tires began spinning on the slick, icy street, and we had some difficulty making our escape as planned, but we finally made it as we watched from an open window and saw them come to the door. We circled back, and approached the house from another direction to cast off suspicion. There in the living room was the family, all standing around the large box. As we passed, we were just able to make out the words on the father's lips as he dug into the bottom of the box: "A turkey!"

Do you get the spirit of the idea? It's one of the grandest, resulting in manifold happiness for the receiver, of course, but also a very special happiness for the giver, *especially* when the giving is anonymous.

Another thought on the subject is brought to mind by an old friend, not of our faith incidentally, but a friend who in his life has naturally felt this same spirit of happiness by giving to others, especially anonymously, even in daily, seemingly insignificant, acts. For example, when he would use a service station rest room, and find the sink extremely dirty and the floor cluttered with paper towels, he would always grab a clean towel, wet it, dab it with soap, and scrub the sink to sparkling clean condition. When leaving, he would pick up all the loose and scattered paper towels on the floor and stuff them tightly into the wastebasket. Just a silent, unknown little act of courtesy, but I have often imagined the thoughts of service station owners when they entered the rest rooms they knew to be dirty, only to find them mysteriously shiny clean and orderly. A great idea.

This same fellow, an ardent antique automobile collector and restorer, has many times come to the aid of his fellow enthusiasts. One man was desperately in need of an old, specially built Model T Ford engine head. My friend found one at an old car swap meet, took it over to the man's car while the owner was at that very moment looking for such an item, secretly placed it on the back floor of the car, and left! I chuckle at the thought of that fellow coming back after an unsuccessful attempt at finding the rare item, only to find it personally delivered to his own car, without further explanation.

There was a very rare pocket watch in my friend's possession, one which reflected the grand era of early automobiles. Diamonds and jewels adorned the fine case work, representing lamps and other such figures. When a very wealthy man, a friend of my friend, indicated his sincere interest in the fine watch, being able, of course, to pay whatever price might be asked, my friend *gave* the watch to him.

The examples are many, and I could go on to magnify the principle of "doing unto others" and befriending someone in need. But the best is simply to try it. Incorporate the concept into your life immediately, and begin to harvest a very wonderful, heart-warming little key to additional happiness in your life.

Fifth Key

*Be creative: always
have a goal.*

Be creative, and express that creativity in always having a goal. Develop special interests—activities to enjoy now and future projects to plan for. These should, of course, include spiritual interests, which I will discuss later, but in this chapter let us consider mainly temporal pursuits.

Long ago I learned that miscellaneous special interests and goals add an important segment of happiness to life. Maybe I derived the idea from an old saying originally uttered by Samuel Smiles over a century ago, "An idle brain is the devil's workshop," to which one could appropriately add, "An idle *life* is also the devil's workshop." The practice of having special interests and goals is so natural that it can easily be adopted early in one's life and continued successfully throughout adulthood. It's a perfect key to happiness for *all* ages, and it can serve the family in times of special need for happiness, when employed either in a joint effort or by individual family members. The results are the same. Individual happiness eventually becomes joint happiness. Happy people get along!

I remember when the concept first came into my own life. I was about six or seven. It began with a great love and admiration for the late Walt Disney's magic world of animated characters. My love for them was so great I wanted to share their presence always. To accomplish this childhood goal, I found myself busily engaged in the evenings, sitting on the living room floor, trying to draw the little characters on 8½-by-11-inch notebook paper. Our bedroom slowly became filled with the drawings. They were not *too* bad, considering my undeveloped graphic sense. Then my brother, two years older than I, and already possessing a definite mind for business, created still another goal. He suggested we go around the neighborhood and sell the drawings. I would produce the product, and he would promote it! It was a good and fun idea, and we made "lots" of money. I think the most costly could be purchased for a formidable three cents. But apart from the money, our young lives were already being made happy through exposure to that needed and important commodity called goals and special interests—in other words, constructive busy-ness, the happiness getter.

Now, to extend the concept a bit further (and also to indulge a secret desire to excite the imagination of young and older readers alike), may I momentarily reflect on the unparalleled grand spirit of childhood, and reminisce by sharing fond memories of later fun times and special interests, together with the happiness I obtained as the concept led gracefully into adulthood.

Interest soon changed from the "Junior Disney Productions" to an overwhelming interest in cowboys, probably spurred on by the Saturday matinees and nearby Knotts Berry Farm. The more my young imagination became exposed to these two influences, the more I thought how wonderful it would be to be a cowboy, especially in a Knotts Berry Farm ghost town *all my own*! The idea began when I was about eight. It's still recorded in my memory as one of the "funnest" projects of my life and, without doubt, one of the happiest!

It started with our old backyard chicken coop. Our very understanding and loving father and mother, after family council, consented to renovate the old building for the realization of our new goal, and the chickens were told they would have to move. A carpenter was commissioned to install a wood floor and a watertight, black, tar paper roof. We even talked him into making a little trapdoor "safe" in the new wood floor. The old chicken coop became the first building of the little ghost town, later named "Stage Valley" by my brother.

The building also had the fame and distinction of becoming the sheriff's office. The first task in furnishing, properly and authentically, the newly renovated office was to negotiate trades with neighborhood kids, acquiring the correct number of needed BB guns. These would assure protection in case of all-out attack by nearby Indians. The guns took their place, lined up on a wall-mounted shelf, over the sheriff's desk. By removing their screw-out barrels, we made an entertaining addition to the adventure: water, poured into the empty barrel assembly, which was then cocked and aimed over the next-door fence at Mrs. Maxwell's chickens, provided great diversion when things got a little boring in "town."

The next building was an old house trailer that had been left in the yard after the passing of my grand-father. He was a grand old man, who, before his death, had agreed to drive the stagecoach when my little town—then in the planning stages—grew and became what I hoped would be competition for Knotts Berry Farm. The proposed name of the intended real-life operation? Black's Berry Farm! We planned on selling blackberry goods instead of boysenberry. Well, the dream at least kept us very happy during those young years.

The old trailer house was turned into the town's hotel. It was big enough to sleep about four kids on Friday night—that is, if we had the courage to stay out in the "old town" the whole night. Stage Valley was growing. Next, construction began on a town bank. Before laying the flooring boards, we dug a one-foot-deep "basement," to be used to hide a man if necessary. We picked up an old cash register at the secondhand store for $1.50, and the sound of its old bell added a great deal of realism and fun.

It seemed back in those days there were lots of good things thrown away, but we soon learned that we had to be the first kids out on Saturday morning to get the "best stuff." I recall walking down our favorite alley where the best treasures were usually found, and my boyhood friend Ralph and I saw "today's find" at the same time. We knew it was to be a first-come-first-served deal; so we both started running toward the pile simultaneously. The treasure this day was a beautiful and very old collection of stuffed birds and deer heads! I grabbed two deer heads and a couple of wild ducks, and Ralph got a beautiful, full-open-spread American Eagle, plus a couple of other small stuffed birds. It was a grand day of junking.

On another occasion, we found, and laboriously lugged home, an old packing crate, which became the town's printing company. The company was responsible for printing the name of the town on all the toy paper money we had purchased from the dime store, the monthly newspaper, and all town announcements and "wanted" posters. Our press was a little toy rubber printing set. Our dating system was current, minus exactly 100 years.

Another crate was obtained for the barber shop, and a huge, old barrel hoisted atop it, simulating the town's water supply. The bank later added a second story, which became the sheriff's personal apartment. This building was particularly fun, even though on windy days it did sway a bit. As the town's first sheriff, I remember the pride I took in placing red cowboy-type scarves in the windows for curtains and a real deer hide in the doorway for a door. Deer hides were a rarity in Los Angeles. Just outside my door, there was a little wood handrail and a narrow porch. Entrance was made by a ladder leaning against the wall closest to the sheriff's office.

A hitching post was placed in front of the hotel, along with a "town fireplace"—a little hole dug to have a campfire on Friday night and to cook breakfast on Saturday morning. Next, a stagecoach office was erected from old boards collected around the neighborhood, and we used another good boyfriend's wagon for the stagecoach. Melvin's wagon was perfect, as it was one of the old wooden frame type that would bend authentically over bumps and ruts. It also looked the best going over Mrs. Maxwell's front yard retaining wall and crashing down into the street below. We used to wonder why Melvin's mother, shaking her rugs across the street and observing the whole thing, would faithfully call Melvin home about that time and have him bring his wagon with him.

The town grew, and so did imagination. A saloon

went up next, with a private back room for the "boss." (Only soft drinks were permitted. It was a friendly town.) On the dirt floor of the boss's office was an old green cushion over a wood frame, flush on the ground. It represented the boss's overstuffed chair. But the real secret was that under the cushion was the entrance to a secret undergound tunnel leading from the saloon, under the town's stage (for the "performing arts"), to the abandoned warehouse next door to the sheriff's office. (The warehouse was straight down First Street; the sheriff's office was located on Main Street; the saloon on Stage Coach Road.) The warehouse was a huge, five-by-five-by-eight-foot wooden crate. I recall it took us half a day to get the thing home. Inside, it was very nicely equipped with one of the first battery-operated portable radios, an extra cap gun, a candle, and lots of soda crackers.

Once in a fierce gunfight, Bobby Martin (one of the most realistic players in town) and I were having it out with a couple of other kids visiting the town for the first time. They were out in the street, and we were in the saloon, trapped! They began tossing dusty, dry, choking "dirt bombs" through the cracks of the wall of the building; so we went into the back room, raised the cushion, and dropped down into the tunnel. We carefully placed the cushion over the opening above us and crawled to safety under the ground and up into the warehouse. As we muffled our laughter, we watched through the cracks in the walls as our enemy continued to bombard the old saloon, threatening to come in and get us any moment if we didn't give up. They probably wondered how we could ever endure so much flying dirt. Finally, with courage unparalleled and dirt everywhere, they rushed the building, only to find it very empty and very, very dusty. That was one of the most fun memories of the "gunfighting" days of Stage Valley.

A daring, three-story apartment house went up next door to the saloon. On the two upper floors we nailed signs reading, "No Entrance, Unsafe," which only served as a decoy to preserve the upper floors for additional secret hiding places. We should have taken heed, however, to our own warning. That old building swayed and creaked every time a slight breeze came along. In front of the hotel was Second Street, which also became the stage route. With the addition of candle-burning streetlights, another tunnel leading under the street from the newly built gun shop to the bank, stones painted gold for the stagecoach strong box, and a hangmen's noose in the old fig tree as a warning to troublemakers, Stage Valley continued until I reached the ripe old age of fourteen.

What a lot of fun—all because of a little goal and some imagination, coupled with hard work. Even to this day the silent, wonderful memory still lives, especially when I recall the little town at night, with all its tiny streetlights flickering from shops and street corners. You young people, think about that. The fun enjoyed from that one goal is still a rich source of happiness, not to speak of all the possible trouble it helped me to avoid during those particular years of my life. The important point is, however, that the concept is valid for *all* ages and subjects.

This adventure, by the way, was forcibly terminated when I was ordered by the city fire department to tear it down because it was a fire hazard. As sheriff of the town, I appealed that order to the chief of the fire department, but the appeal was denied and Stage Valley was sadly torn down.

After recovering for several months from the sorrow of losing the town, I regained my composure and began another goal for happiness—collecting antiques. Those were the days when the shelves of a secondhand store were filled with real treasures, costing about a dollar—for example, women's high-top, buttoned shoes for $1.25. Over the years my antique collection evolved from swords and old guns to World War II German helmets, and eventually became a very lovely antique pocket watch collection, including meticulously handmade specimens dating back to 1725!

I enjoyed this collection for a few years, and it later became the trading stock for a family project—a 1911 Model T Ford Commercial Roadster, fully restored, which we presently own, and which, incidentally, after many years, still has the very same ignition switch given me as a boy while I was cleaning out a friend's garage. At that time I dreamed of one day having the car to put it on. It was a little, secret goal all of its own, now a reality.

Now another example of a possible happiness goal in your life. Once I thought how fun it would be to save as much money as I could. I set a goal of an amazing $2,000. On a piece of art stock I drew a large thermometer, with increment lines of $50 each and a total of $2,000 indicated at the top. Each time I saved $50, I filled in another increment with red pencil. It began to rise. If I desired to go to the movies, I put the corresponding amount into a little bank and spent the evening instead watching television or enjoying some other activity. If my car was due for repair I checked the estimated cost, purchased the parts, and did the repair myself, putting the amount saved into my bank.

This went on for about a year and a half, and at last the goal was achieved. $2,000! Now that I had the money, I didn't know what to do with it! Deciding on some kind of wise investment, I went out to a fairly nice neighborhood nearby and found a house appearing to be quite unkept. An old stove and washing machine and four junk cars adorned the front yard, together with an old mattress. With some difficulty I found the front door hidden behind a camouflage of thick bamboo trees, and knocked. The owner came to the door, and I asked him if he might be interested in selling his house and moving. Surprisingly, he said yes. We negotiated and agreed on a purchase price of $13,000, with a $1,000 down payment and assumption of a G.I. loan at 4½ percent interest. He agreed to vacate the premises in one month.

Now what to do with the other $1,000? I thought how wonderful it would be to return to Denmark, land of my forefathers and my mission. I checked with the airlines and found the cost of one roundtrip ticket to be a shocking $850. That was too much for me. Checking around I found a ski club planning a European ski tour to Switzerland. The cost? A meager $220 for the round trip! I questioned further to see if participants were required to be skiers. I was glad they weren't, for I had never been on skis in my life. I made the trip, with more than enough extra cash for fun.

While I enjoyed the wonderful, tiny kingdom of Denmark, another little goal was in a small way started: a possible Danish Import Giftware Shop and America's only Danish Museum. Together with lots of reacquainting and fun, time was also well spent in making potential business contacts, and in much sketching, note-taking, research, and taking pictures of Danish artifacts in museums, together with as much purchasing of Danish antiquities as possible.

Returning home, broke but with a house, I commenced slowly putting the ugly duckling of the neighborhood back into repair and beauty. It was a fun project, with new paneling, painting, wall papering, and so forth. I chuckled when I found the mysterious hump in the back yard to be a complete, grass-covered, hand-laid brick floor of a patio! The bamboo was removed in the front, along with a section of the front wall. Double-entry doors were then installed, complementing the front of the house. The old place was taking shape. Trees—given by a friend—were planted, grass carefully cut and styled, and decorative chipped bark spread out. The outside was painted, a modern porch light fixture was carefully hung in place, and the ugly duckling was soon accepted and praised by kind neighbors all around.

With plans for my little business still flickering in

my heart, I put the house up for sale at a competitive $19,500—$6,500 over the purchase price. I sold the house almost immediately and invested the difference, mostly profit, in my next goal of self employment: a three-fold enterprise, including a Danish Import Gift Shop, America's only Danish Museum, and a Bicycle Rental, all to be located in the charming Danish capital of the United States, the little village of Solvang, California. The dream materialized into one of the most pleasant, rewarding experiences of my life. In that quaint, lovely area I also had the privilege of initiating the first Church seminary program. From that choice experience alone came many of my very best friendships, not to mention several new young members of the Church. All this because of a dream, a goal, and some hard, but most enjoyable work.

Now another look at special goals, interests, hobbies, and so forth. There ofttimes is a certain magic about having a special interest or goal in your life. The late President David O. McKay, in writing to seminary and institute people, explicitly emphasized the need for other interests in our lives beyond the scope of our daily careers. He spoke of the need for correct balance of the temporal and spiritual things in life, exemplified in his own lifelong varied interests, such as his love of the horses and farm which he owned at Huntsville. It is my strong conviction that men and women, boys and girls also need the daily change of pace that comes with other interests in life besides their normal daily tasks, duties, career, and religion. Not only do other interests give pleasure while one actively participates in them, but the thought of them alone provides untold happiness and comfort. What a simple but very successful therapy for bad days at the office, in the home, or whatever— just the thought of something loved, pleasing, and personally yours, something you are master of.

Now, to derive further happiness from special goals and interests, allow me to introduce a law I have entitled "The Law of Substitution and Creativity."

63

(Sounds rather impressive, doesn't it?) Essentially, it has to do with those in a lower income bracket who have desires for some temporal wealth but also a commitment to more fundamental values, such as their religious convictions and their families. The "substitution" part of the law has to do with substituting the real thing wanted with something close, yet not quite the same, which would do the job.

Example: My wife and I really wanted a nice camper for family outings, travel, and so forth. We wanted the type that housed the cab with the camper section, enabling us to walk from the front driving seats to the actual camper area without having to stop the vehicle. Realizing, however, that we would be unable to afford such a luxury "travel home," we applied the "law of substitution" by going to a government-sponsored auction of government vehicles. We looked over the long list of vehicles to be auctioned, planned for the particular one we desired, and submitted our bid, adding one dollar over the price we wanted to pay. Wanting to pay $200, we bid $201 on a large three-quarter-ton ex-mail van, the perfect size for a camper. We won the bid at $201.

We then put into effect the second part of the law, the "law of creativity." This we applied to the planning and decorating of the interior. We made it a family project, with both my wife and I working on it in the evenings. In a few fun months, we finished the interior, complete with a baby bed in an area near the driver, previously reserved for small packages, and a built-in olive green double sink, bought on sale at a trailer supply store. The sink had a small chip in the enamel, but a dab of touch-up paint rendered it barely noticeable. We installed a lovely four-burner gas range, a large icebox (also bought on sale, slightly blemished), a perfectly functioning chemical toilet of our own design, a small closet, and bench-type upholstered chairs with a drop-down table in the rear, which at night could easily be converted into a comfortable, nearly full-sized bed!

In our new camper (which, incidentally, cost us far

less than the *sales tax* on the "real" thing) we also enjoy the unusual features of a translucent glass ceiling, allowing natural light to shine into the camper by day, and a full rear wall that can be unlocked, raised, and neatly folded into the ceiling, lending complete open-air pleasure, especially impressive when this open back door faces the beauty of a lake, a river, a canyon, or a campfire slowly burning itself out as the night grows late.

It's a fun law, and surely enables those less endowed financially, or those who are simply thrifty, to enjoy some of life's temporal pleasures, once thought of as "just for others." This same law occasionally can apply to shrimp instead of lobster, good quality hamburger instead of steak, an antiqued photo reproduction of an original Book of Mormon, a beautiful collection of plastic "rare old guns," or, if it can't be a Porsche, a nice VW, and so on. If you don't think you can have it, try the simple, yet very fun, law of substitution and creativity. Substitute for the real thing, and be creative in its needed improvement or change. The whole idea can add to life a lot of old-fashioned happiness, previously untapped.

Now a little further enlightenment on this same trend of thought. Most men see an area of psychological unknown in women, and vice versa. I recall many years ago going into a little shop and seeing a fairly large, hardbound copy of a book entitled "All I Know about Women," by a doctor of one sort or another. With boyish curiosity, spurred on by the "importance" for me to know all about women at the crucial age of sixteen, I picked up the book and began looking through it. To my surprise, the first few pages were completely blank, then the following, and the following! The entire book was filled with blank pages! I laughed at the fact that there was such a thing as a book made with blank pages, but didn't grasp what the author was really saying. Now I laugh again, but with a different understanding of what was just amusing when I was sixteen. The point is, even a woman will agree that there are certain times in her

65

life or things she does that are unexplainable, even to herself—for example, when sudden tears are just necessary. Well, those times are somewhat challenging for us menfolk, as our beloved wives will also testify.

But now on the other side of the coin, I'll try with trembling inadequacy to explain a common segment of the man's inscrutable side. With the daily pressure of providing comes the need for periodic moments of escape. Among the temporal means by which these are obtained are a man's very special interests, often misunderstood by his helpmate. An example, I suppose about as unfathomable as a wife who has to cry for no obvious reason, is the husband who buys a deactivated World War II Nazi submachine gun. In some strange way, is it perhaps the boy of the man coming out? Or is it the indefinable cry for special identification of masculinity? Don't try to find a logical reason for such an action, for there will more than likely be none. This is possibly a time in his life when he too needs an area of comfort. Whatever the reason, if the thing desired fills that void in a man's or a woman's system, let's be grateful for such simple therapy, especially when it results in direct fulfillment of happiness in one of the mysterious areas of human life.

A prerequisite for this reasoning, though, is, of course, to use wisdom and common sense. I can still remember the reaction of my dear wife when I came into the kitchen from the living room holding my hurting right eye. I hesitated to tell her right away that while trying to make the experience of running my electric train around the Christmas tree even more realistic, I lay on the floor, face on the carpet, one eye squinted, watching the single ray of its cute little light slowly chugging up the track. And while I was so enthralled by the realism of the moment, the train hit me right in the eye!

Have a goal—one to pursue actively now and one to plan for the future—one sure key to happiness!

Sixth
Key

*Maintain a wholesome relationship
with the opposite sex.*

Maintain a wholesome relationship with the opposite sex. Cheating morally is probably one of the most promising ways to personal unhappiness. The Lord incorporated in man a fine line between happiness and unhappiness, depending upon whether man honors the law of virtue or not. This law is prerequisite to major happiness in our lives, whether we are married or single. It applies to all who are in love or who are mature enough to have a normal attraction for the opposite sex.

This chapter will be geared primarily to those younger and less experienced in dating, specifically teens, but with a definite overtone of warning for all physically mature men and women and boys and girls, married or unmarried. Years ago, while I was still in high school, there was a girl named Cheryl, whom I admired greatly, but to whom I also felt inferior. Cheryl was the type who was busily engaged in every form of constructive activity. She was the ward choir director, a pianist, active in most auxiliaries, and vice-president of the high school; and she even put on her own vocal concerts. She was quite the girl and I liked her. But during our high school years I never got up enough courage to ask her for a date.

This hidden wish went on for some three years, until finally it was all over for the good old alma mater. We were at last graduating seniors. Following graduation exercises the class was attending a little party, at which Cheryl and I found ourselves sitting next to each other during the evening's activities. Sipping fruit punch, I turned to her and mustered up enough courage to say something to the effect, "Well, Cheryl, it's all over. High school is all behind us now." I continued with, "You know what? I think I now have enough courage to tell you something I've wanted to for three long years." She asked what that could possibly be, and I replied, "I've wanted to ask you out on a date for three long years!"

She turned to me, suddenly stopped sipping her punch, and said, "Oh no! Do you want to know something else?" I did, and she said, "For three long years I've wanted you to ask me out!"

As we both registered some amusement at our predicament, I leaned over to her and said, "Cheryl, I have an idea."

"What is it?" she said.

"Let's go out!" I replied, quickly and emphatically. She accepted, and we went on a date belated by three years.

Now this was not my first successful, fun date with a girl, but it served well as a last high school memory and a reminder of that special kind of date I have since entitled a "neck-up" date, rather than a "neckdown" date. Why the unusual title? Well, a date with a girl like Cheryl is an evening filled with one clean,

happy, fun-promoting activity after another. It is a date which depends on personality and spirit, rather than the pressures, ugliness, and eventual serious unhappiness of making out, light petting, and so on. I have told many boys another way of looking at it: "If you can't remember after the date what she looked like from the neck down, there is a good chance it was a successful date!" In other words, let the dating concept in your life be a sparkling, easy, fun-promoting one. Don't allow the temptations of physical attraction to ruin not only the date, but also very likely your new friendship and your future spiritual standing. It will never happen if you concentrate on a neck-up kind of date. Let a good spirit preside in your dating memories, rather than the depression that comes from wishing you hadn't made the wrong decision. Much testimony has been shared with me as to the often gross unhappiness that comes to a couple who catch themselves in the snare of Satan's obvious trap of physical involvement: lots of worry, eventual loss of self-respect, loss of virtue, and finally the crushing danger of loss of testimony. I thank Cheryl for reminding us of the important concepts of neck-up dating.

I had a young student some years ago by the name of Donna. She carried on the same concept and added in her testimony one day, "How neat it is to get up in the morning feeling unashamed of the previous evening's activities." It's a great joy to come in from the date, whether boy or girl, and in the privacy of your own spirit, take a long, deep look into the mirror and congratulate yourself that you and your date maintained respect for each other. The apostle LeGrand Richards has often said, "The eyes are the mirrors of the soul." Have you ever looked into your own eyes after sinning? They really tell the story, don't they? Have you ever really noticed a person's eyes when he is really happy? They really tell another story, don't they?

Many years ago, just about the time I was showing an interest in dating, my brother took me to one side and with great interest and brotherly love advised me, "Be different, and always treat her like a queen." I liked the advice, but also found the consequences of it to be very valuable. To treat a girl like a queen has many favorable results: your personal gratification for having fully respected her—and therefore greater depth and enjoyment in the dating experience—and her respect for you in turn. But not to be overlooked is that feeling of importance. When one is treated like royalty—a king or queen—one has greater desire to *be* like royalty. Thus one person's good actions have influenced the other's. Purity is contagious. (Tiny tip: For best results and a guarantee of being treated like a king or queen, *be worthy of it*. You qualify for what you're qualified for.)

Now there is another important concept in improving your dating and maintaining a good relationship with the opposite sex. It is in harmony with the ideas previously mentioned, but is *the* most important ingredient for wholesome dating. I call it the "three or five concept." Make it a three or five date. If there are just two of you going on the date this evening, invite your Heavenly Father to be with you, making a total of *three* going. If it's to be a double date, also invite your Heavenly Father to go along with you, making it five altogether. Why take your Heavenly Father along on a date? Well, since he has very probably already experienced these same things many years ago on his earth, he is the most reliable source of understanding and love to guide us through life's many pathways successfully. Hence, he *is* our Father and we literally his children. Kids go to parents for help and advice; let's go to him. Even better, let's ask him to go along with us. Think about that. Who would be tempted to fool around, with God sitting right between him and his date?

Learn some spiritual defense strategy. A young girl named Candace once told me of an incident in which the date she was "not enjoying" was trying his tactics of making common that which should be kept sacred. Noticing her discomfiture as she wondered how to

cope with his obvious intentions of intimacy, he
asked her what the matter was. Simply, sweetly, and
very emphatically, she recited the thirteenth Article
of Faith. Calling him by name, she said, "We believe
in being honest, true, chaste, benevolent, virtuous,
and in doing good to all men; indeed, we may say
that we follow the admonition of Paul—We believe all
things, we hope all things, we have endured many
things, and hope to be able to endure all things. If
there is anything virtuous, lovely, or of good report
or praiseworthy, we seek after these things." What
fellow or girl, after such a powerful dissertation on
cleanliness, would any longer have unclean thoughts?
Candace's friend lost all interest in his earlier objec-
tive.

Memorize these inspired words, my young brothers
and sisters. They may save your life.

Through the years I have had both the sorrow and
the enjoyment of hearing from kids about their dates.
Some dates have been overwhelmingly fun-filled, with
no overtones of evil; but there have been the others,
sinful and ugly, characterized by activity which has
caused even our young men to come home and
remorsefully think about it so deeply that they too
have cried themselves to sleep pondering the dilemma. There is no comparison between a spiritual
date and one of the body only. Learn this important
concept now, while young and lovely, unspotted and
clean. Be worthy of the best. Know well the warning
given in section 10 of the Doctrine and Covenants.
Satan and his followers desire darkness over light. No
wonder it's so easy to sin at night. No wonder so
much crime and loss of virtue take place after dark.
That's Satan's strongest time of attack. Now we can
better understand why Jesus is called the light. Light
is truth.

Now may I share my personal testimony with you
to emphasize these sacred thoughts. When I first
became acquainted with my wife, Ann, and felt
myself falling in love little by little, I immediately
took time out in the new-forming friendship to do

some serious soul searching, with deep thinking. I
wanted so badly *not* to allow this special, blossoming
friendship to be made common, as dating so often
becomes. I did want to "be different," as my brother
many years ago had so wisely counseled.

We dated, we laughed, we sang, we talked. It was
true. We were falling in love, and neither of us could
deny it. But maybe, at this particular time, even more
important was the fact that we were becoming
friends. Why even more important? Well, after much
thought on that subject alone I came to the simple
conclusion that it was so much more appropriate and
important to be falling in love with a friend! So an
important concept was learned. Make it a friendship
first, then a romance. Our friendship grew; carefully
trailing, so did the romance. Oh, I wanted to kiss her
good-night following our first date. But that's the
very start of making a romance common. We didn't
want that. If we were seriously in love, we didn't
want *anything* to cheat us of the opportunity of
finding out correctly.

I remember on the fourth date we walked up to
her door to say good night. I believe the porch light
was on. By this time in our young friendship there
were definite evidences seeping through our hearts
that the friendship was evolving into young love. It
was! We knew that. It was manifest to us while we
were together and alone. At the close of this particular date, wanting to know that my affection was real
and becoming more serious in a mature way, I held
her hand softly, gave it an extra tender but light
squeeze, placed my cheek to hers, and said good
night. Our eyes spoke for our hearts. Our spirits
communicated. It was far more than what physical
communication could have rendered.

It wasn't until our fifth date that we kissed. Let me
tell you just a little about those circumstances. It was
an experience I will never forget. Yes, it was just a
kiss, but nonetheless a kiss unlike that common
among many young people, for it was even sacred.

We had just returned from a date. I walked Ann up

to the door to say our last good night before departing. She informed me that her father and mother were out and that she would feel much better if I would wait a few minutes until she was ready to retire. I agreed and waited in the living room. Ann came back some minutes later, and asked if we could have a closing prayer to end our date. I thought it was a sweet thought, and I agreed. We knelt together and told our Heavenly Father how privileged we felt for finding each other, and for our friendship which both of us now realized was progressing into a lovely romance, sacred in nature. I told Heavenly Father how honored I was for her love, for her goodness. It was a spiritually thrilling occurrence. We closed by asking him to guard and guide our new love. Upon uttering the word *amen*, we turned to each other on bended knee, before the presence of our Father, and then, at last, it was made known to us that the special time had come. We embraced, and we kissed for the first time.

Only heavenly words could describe that experience. It was in all truthfulness heavenly, even indescribable in earthly terms. Oh, what a far cry from the common approach to the same experience. Can you see the difference between having and not having the spirit in dating? That beautiful experience was, to a great extent, an answer to our other prayers as to whether or not we were really in love—you know, the kind of love that leads to engagement and marriage. Kids ask me all the time, "How will we really know if our love is enough for marriage?" The answer again is: by our Father *telling* us through the spirit, after we've asked. This reply is given to each personally, if both are worthy of the communication. (More on this in the Seventh Key, following.) Oh yes, make it a neck-up date. Make it a three or five date. Make it a date the memory of which you can share with *your* kids someday during home evening—*your* home evening.

Now in closing this very important key to happiness, let me make one more attempt at clarifying the sacredness of dating and relationships with the opposite sex. My younger brothers, let us put into our minds this analogy of our dating partners. Let us compare them to the loveliness of the flower so overwhelmingly white, fragrant, and pure—the gardenia. Isn't it without doubt one of the most beautiful floral creations of our Father in heaven? But have you ever seen such a flower when it is taken from its cool, fresh air? Have you seen what happens to its beauty when it is exposed to warm, humid air and touched along the edge of its petals? It turns brown and begins to wilt. It loses its lovely fragrance and beauty, and slowly begins to die. After a while, even he who possesses it is no longer happy with its presence. Think about that, my brothers. Think about that, my sisters. Don't be responsible for your guy's fall. Help him help both of you. Make your future kids proud of their parents—you!

Dads and moms, stay true to the covenants entered into through marriage. Surreptitious flirtations and secret "friendships" with members of the opposite sex are, in reality, not-so-secret stepping stones to great and serious loss in this life and also in the great life to come. Remember, though the secret heart-throb in comparison to your mate may seem so much more perfect or delightful to behold, how could there be any truth or God-sent spirit in such a relationship, founded upon cheating and defiling of body and spirit, plus dishonor of the most important quality of love: trust? How could you ever really trust each other when one or both cheated in making the initial acquaintance? Could such a relationship really have anything to do with mature love? Better, sit down with your beloved, whom you chose with that special feeling of love years ago. Discuss the problems intelligently, softly, together, and then with your Father, who will most likely by this time already have come into your presence. Take the opportunity to exercise your faith, and in so doing smite Satan, rather than voluntarily joining him. Bind your love stronger through the experience, instead of weakening it and eventually destroying it with such tools of Satan as flattery, deceit, hate, and lack of self-control. Husbands, start dating your wives again. Let each day include the words "I love you."

God bless you all to find the great importance and happiness in this basic key of life given us just for the living of it. Bask in the warming, soothing rays of moral cleanliness. Let not Satan's influence of moral degradation come near your lives. God lives. His gospel is true, even in dating. Be true to it.

Seventh Key

Get to know and trust your Heavenly Father as a close, personal friend.

Get to know your Heavenly Father as a close, personal friend, and then trust him just that way. This seventh and last key of happiness is probably the most important of all.

In achieving this close, personal relationship, prayer is the prime requisite. Many utter prayers from their lips daily. Fewer from their hearts. That's the problem. The boy prophet Joseph was forewarned of this weakness in man during his first holy conversation with the Father and the Son in the grove on that chosen day. Despite prophetic warning, the problem is still with us. While on his mission Jesus warned of the same dilemma. He cautioned against using vain repetition and praying without sincerity or privacy, to be heard of man only. He even gave us a structured outline to follow, now commonly known as the Lord's Prayer.

Sincerity is one of the main keys to a close and intimate relationship with our Father. Be careful of falling for trite phrases which are learned and uttered on the tip of the tongue but far from the heart. We sometimes learn a good-sounding phrase and memorize it, with little or no sincerity. We all have heard the ones used most: "bless this food that it will nourish and strengthen our bodies"; "bless our teacher that he (or she) will have a good lesson prepared for us . . . that we'll be able to use it in our daily lives"; "bless us with all those things thou seest we stand in need of"; "bless all those who are not here this time that they will be able to be here next time" (By the way, this one was recently heard uttered in a church meeting held in the Utah State Prison.); ". . . that no harm or accident will befall us"; et cetera, et cetera, et cetera.

Now there is nothing wrong with any of the above phrases, *if* they are from the heart and not from the lips only. But too many of us seem to learn them well enough that we can fluently fill an entire prayer with them, all in about two breaths. This is one of the things Jesus was referring to when he spoke of "vain repetitions." Use caution and sincerity. If it's *you* saying it, then repetition is fine. If it's just a well-learned and thoughtless set of words in your prayer vocabulary, try it again, but this time all alone, in *your* words, and welcome to a wonderful, new sacred experience with prayer and very possibly a much closer, more loving relationship with our Heavenly Father.

Take a closer look at your relationship with him, and see where you really stand. I imagine many "prayers" have begun after the pillow has been fluffed up and the blankets pulled comfortably around the neck: the words "Heavenly Father" have escaped, and that's about all, as a tired body cancelled out the rest of that possible holy communication. Maybe we need to review in our minds that we are about to *really* communicate with our Father for a few minutes, and that it's serious spiritual business to call his attention from other matters in order to converse with him. Make it a real, living experience, not just a moment of the day finally to ponder over all the little things: Did I put out the trash? Is that the kitchen sink or the bathroom sink that's dripping? Is the dog outside? I wonder if he loves me. Yuk, an algebra test tomorrow! And so on. Someone has said that when we pray it should be such a real experience that we would want to take a little peak while praying, wondering if the Lord had not actually come into the room during the conversation.

A few moments of mind clearing is a good idea prior to addressing our Father. Some call it meditating; some, getting into the mood or spirit. It's a spiritual pause, a time to think. Have your prayer; then after conversing with him, *stay down* for a few moments for a possible direct reply. Believe in what you have just done! It seems common for us to ask for a whole list of needed things, then utter the word "Amen," jump up, and start whatever we were about to do just prior to praying. It would be interesting to see the other side of the experience sometime. Maybe we would see a patient, loving Father ready to sit down to an evening's rest and relaxation, when

suddenly on the prayer meter our prayer comes through. He sits and listens carefully to the entire list of needs, notes those able to be given immediately, logs the others, then waits for the end of the prayer to answer it. Just as he is about to influence the experience with a lovely feeling of acknowledgment, he hears the "Amen," and up we jump and go on our way, leaving our Father, whom we have just asked for special favors, standing there with the blessings ready to give but with no one to give them to. I think the moments *after* a prayer can ofttimes be the most special and sacred of the experience. Think about that.

Another thought on the subject. Have you ever wondered why the Lord many times has made reference to the necessity of being like little children? Well, the answer seems to reflect their simple belief and sincerity. If a child loses a nickle, he asks Heavenly Father to help him find it. Would an adult do that? Yes, in some cases, but not too often. An adult often considers such an experience too trite to bother about it, when in reality it is a perfect chance for a little faith-promoting miracle in his life.

Another means of increasing the closeness of the relationship with our Father is to give him credit when a blessing or a direct response to an inquiry is given. How many times do we automatically feel, "Well, even though it's exactly what I asked for, it probably would have happened that way anyway, without the prayer"? I wonder how our Father feels about those thoughts. How would *you* feel if you were the giver? We ask, he gives, we doubt it. It reminds me of the story of the little boy who found himself slipping off the roof of a barn and quickly uttered a prayer asking Heavenly Father to help him. The next moment the little boy's trousers caught on a nail, stopping him from his fall, and he continued, "Never mind, a *nail* stopped me!" Giving our Father the credit is giving us the faith. Isn't the folly that coincidence is the answer clearly a bold play by Satan to deflect the credit from where it is due, cheat us of a warm experience with our faith, destroy a nice opportunity to build personal testimony, and rob us of the opportunity to share the experience with someone weak in spirit? The apostle LeGrand Richards used to say, "When in doubt about tithing, pay it!" The same philosophy can be aptly applied to answer to prayer: "When in doubt about the origin of the answer, give the credit to the Lord. Matthew (chapter 10, verses 29-31) relates that our Heavenly Father even notices the little sparrow which has fallen to the ground. This is vivid and intimate evidence of the Lord's true feelings regarding the importance of all matters upon this earth. He loves and cares for us in the most minute degree.

An important word of caution, however. When a person is sinning regularly, his desire to pray usually stops. This is dangerous. Prayer, if sincere, is one of the sweetest spiritual experiences and helps God has given man. It is, in all reality, our lifeline.

I recall a story involving sincere prayer and a young man named Steve Hall. He was a big boy, about 200 pounds, and a rough and tough ball player in high school. He was not a member of the Church, but dated a sweet young LDS girl. Desiring to share with him that which excited her about the Church, she arranged for two young missionaries to come over and introduce the principles of the gospel to him. They told him enthusiastically about the boy prophet Joseph and his seeing the Father and the Son, literally present there in a grove of trees. At the close of the discussion, the elders bore to him their testimonies, indicating that they knew without doubt in their minds that the story related to him was true, adding that now it was up to him to find out for himself. Their testimonies and their discussion were only guides to follow; in the end he personally would have to find out whether the story told him was true or not. If it was true, it was the greatest story ever told since shepherds watched their sheep that blissful night nearly two thousand years ago; if not, Mormonism made one of the most monstrously fallacious

85

claims of all Christian religions. The elders made Steve promise that he would personally ask his Heavenly Father about what they had told him of the boy prophet, Joseph, and he committed himself to them, his girl friend, and the Lord.

That night, when retiring, he jumped into bed, fluffed up the pillow, got the blankets arranged just as they should be for overall, relaxed comfort, and then it hit him. He began to be haunted by his last reply to the elders, "Yes, I will. I'll kneel down and ask God." He thought about his commitment, made his decision, and threw off the blankets, and all 200 pounds of that boy rolled out of bed onto his knees in prayer position. Steve had never prayed vocally before, but his commitment to the elders included verbal prayer. Alone in the room, he looked around, feeling a bit odd at the idea of addressing someone he couldn't see, but commenced nevertheless. He later shared the words of that prayer with me. They were, in essence, "Heavenly Father, this is Steve Hall. I was talking to some young men in the Mormon Church and they told me some pretty heavy things. They asked me to ask you if it was true, and they said it would make a lot of difference in my life if it was. Heavenly Father, wherever you are, did Joseph Smith really see you and . . ." That's all that made it out of that great big guy's heart. He couldn't say any more, because a strange feeling he had never had before came over his being. A large lump filled his throat, and tears streamed down his face. Big Steve was crying; yet he had never felt so good inside. He was encountering that very sublime experience of actually communicating with our Father and having the sweetness of the Holy Ghost about him. That's what it's all about. Believing in God so much that we ask him directly about things that trouble us—and get an answer. Sometimes the answer is given later, serving as a little challenge to our faith while we're waiting. Section 9, verse 8, of the Doctrine and Covenants tells about it very plainly:

*But, behold, I say unto you, that you must study it
out in your mind; then you must ask me if it be right,
and if it is right I will cause that your bosom shall
burn within you; therefore, you shall feel that it is
right.*

Alma also spoke of things relating to this passage:

*Yea, and cry unto God for all thy support; yea, let
all thy doings be unto the Lord, and whithersoever
thou goest let it be in the Lord; yea, let thy thoughts
be directed unto the Lord; yea, let the affections of
thy heart be placed upon the Lord forever.*
*Counsel with the Lord in all thy doings, and he will
direct thee for good; yea, when thou liest down at
night lie down unto the Lord.* (Alma 37:36-37.)

I suppose this prophet and others, through their
close association with the Lord, are saying, in other
words, "Get up and do something about your beliefs.
Act upon them; pray about them." Today we might
say, "Turn on spiritually," and rightfully add the
admonition to get rid of the "preventers"—the things
in life that continually hold us back in a greater or
lesser degree from attaining true spirituality: things
like lying just a little, cheating a little, feeling justified
in viewing rated movies, and so forth.

Recently, at a family get-together, a very enjoyable
discussion took place regarding family members'
views on various subjects relating to gospel ideals and
principles. As the subjects and the hours passed, we
landed momentarily on the pros and cons of Church
members watching rated movies. We have a young
cousin in our family, who is both very intelligent and
delightful to be around. He, his charming wife, and
some other family members took one side of the
discussion and a few of us the other. We discussed the
issues quite thoroughly. Basically, their feelings at the
time were that as members of the true Church we
should be able to be open-minded enough to take

87

into our lives the whole spectrum of life, whether it be negative or positive, since all of life's experiences will eventually take their place of benefit in our overall makeup and development. The other side contended that full development of character and spirit does not need voluntary exposure to the negative. There was plenty of it without asking and paying for more. Both sides finally retired to their corners, and the debate ended with handshakes, and smiles, and good-byes until next year. But still each left with a deeper thought of the real issue still unfinished.

Weeks passed, and Ann and I received a most lovely letter from our cousins. I would like to share a few lines from it. The emphasis added is mine.

Since that night over at the family's I have thought a lot about the things you and I were talking about. Much has become clearer to me. I have been particularly concerned with the problems of movies. The explicit sexual scenes, anti-gospel themes, abusive language, and heavy emphasis on physical violence seem very prevalent. In fact, there are hardly any movies without them. In reading through conference reports from the October conference, however, I find mention made several times, in very specific ways, of these kinds of movies, and a strong condemnation by Harold B. Lee of R and X rated films. Although I find much of value in movies like ——, ——, ——, and —— (all rated R), I think that what the Brethren are saying is this: If you're really serious about becoming pure in heart, then the harm which these movies cause to you personally far outweighs the good which you receive. *My conclusion then is that although much can be gained from many of today's movies, much more can be lost by the effects of the explicit sex scenes and anti-gospel themes upon a person's mind and spirit. As a consequence, we have given up all R and X rated films. And we're just about to the point (after seeing —— and being disappointed) of forgetting most of the GP films too.*

I hope you don't mind wading through this long

diatribe, but it represents for us some new insights, and I just wanted to share them with you.

Love,

———————

Much more could be said regarding other "preventers," including immodest dress (a preventer of good spirit for both the wearer and the watcher), foul language, out-of-spirit reading material and humor, and so on. But I think the point is clear. The preventers obstruct true spiritual communication and development, causing a lack of warm tones and tiny miracles in our lives. The extent to which we permit this interference is our own personal decision alone.

I'm very fond of Alma's passage encouraging us to get closer to the Lord "for all thy support" (37:36). I like that. In the very truest sense, he is offering us the greatest insurance policy ever. And to validate any claims, all that is required is personal worthiness and a close relationship with him who allowed us to experience this earthly time of test. For years my personal testimony has been enriched and amazed at the vast scope of Alma's challenge, given from the Lord.

Let me illustrate. When I was just a boy, hiking in the mountains with others, we suddenly realized it was getting dark. It seems that when it is dark in the mountains it is a special kind of *dark* dark! We continued on the trail, using a small flashlight as our only source of light. I remember the wind was blowing. As the night grew colder, and we more tired and scared, we realized that we were now lost and had missed the main trail. We yelled for help but to no avail.

The oldest with us was the bishop's son. He was about fourteen. He suddenly stopped us on the trail and said, "We're lost, you guys. We better have a prayer." I remember wondering in my young mind, "What good would a prayer do way out here?" We nestled together in a small circle there on the mountainside, and again the oldest boy offered a word of prayer. It was simple and forthright: we were lost and

89

he told the Lord so; we needed help and he asked the Lord for it. A few minutes after we had uttered "Amen" at the close of his prayer, we heard the calling from our family. It came from way up on the mountain down which we were hiking. We called back, and they answered, instructing us to follow the sound of their voices. We did, and slowly made our way up the steep hillside. When we returned safely to our families, the answer to how the Lord could help us in such a predicament was made vividly clear. We asked why our family members had not called out for us before. They informed us that they had, but about fifteen minutes previously there had been a strong wind that apparently had carried the voices the opposite way. That was right about the time we had held our prayer.

Another illustration. Some years later, as a boy about in my mid teens, I already had the great interest in automobiles that would be mine for many years to follow. I had purchased a rare 1924 aluminum-bodied Model T Ford sedan show car, and desired to enter it in a quite famous Southern California car show sponsored by General Motors. There would be 124 cars competing. The car, in my opinion, was perfect for entry. To my dismay, however, a day before the show I noticed transmission slippage, which would require immediate attention. At 4:00 p.m. the day before the show, I started repair procedures on the transmission. My father visited the garage and gave me the encouraging word that the job should normally require about one hour. That was gratifying.

I removed the floor boards from the car, took my position on the concrete floor of the garage, straddling the drive line, and faced the transmission. Removing the inspection-adjustment plate, I separated the bands from the transmission and began the repair by replacing the lining on the bands. Completing this seemingly simple task, I proceeded to replace the newly relined bands in the transmission. Numbers one and two slipped right into place without the slightest problem. Number three was next. It began properly, but then suddenly sprang out of place. I pulled it out and tried again. The same thing occurred. I tried it again and again. I tried using a screwdriver to guide it into place. That didn't work either. Time wore on, and nothing seemed to accomplish the task needed.

About midnight my father came out into the garage and suggested that I come in, reminding me of the late hour. In a discouraged tone I reminded him of my great hope to complete the job that night in order to enter the car in the show the following day. Just as he left me, he pointed out a few new ideas in hopes of helping me. I quickly tried them all, but none seemed to help. I continued to try and try. The night grew on—2:00 a.m. . . . 3:00 a.m. . . . 3:30 . . . quarter to four in the morning. I was tired and disgusted. For nearly twelve hours I had been bending over that transmission. Finally, in near total disgust, I stepped out from the car, took my wrench, aimed carefully at the far end of the garage, and in a full teen-age display of anger, threw that wrench with all the might left in my now very feeble body. I wanted to see it spark as it hit the concrete floor. It did, and buried itself into a dark, obscure corner of the garage. It was all over. I had lost.

I walked outside. It was cold, dark, and dewy. Then it happened. I suppose some dear Sunday School teacher along the way, who probably swore with tears in her eyes about "that Black boy never listening to a word I say," had somehow, miraculously got something through to one of those noisy kids on the back row. Somehow, I had retained a part of a lesson given somewhere, sometime, in my young life. I don't know if it was a voice or just a strong feeling, but something said just as clear as that beautiful sky that night, "Alma said, 'Counsel with the Lord in *all* thy doings.' " Being young, I wondered seriously who in the dickens Alma was! I tried to disregard the message as best I could, but it came through again. I didn't answer aloud, but I remember

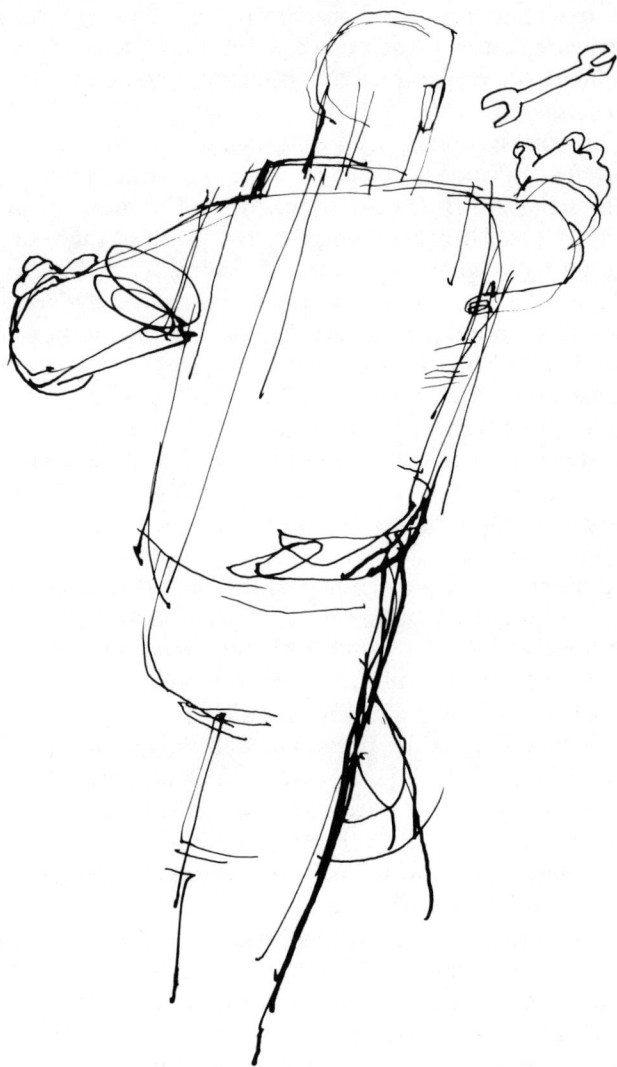

answering finally in my mind, "Fine. Sure. Counsel with the Lord about a *transmission* that needs repair?" The voice or feeling came back with a swift "Why not?" There was a regular, but very strange, "conversation" going on between a young, very spiritually inexperienced kid, and a "pro." We had debated for some time when the challenge was finally put before me forthrightly, "Why don't you try it? Ask your Heavenly Father for help—*now!*"

Well, this whole experience was a bit humbling to say the least. I looked around the back yard to see if anyone was watching me. I guess I wasn't too surprised at not seeing anyone out mowing his lawn, weeding, or something. It was close to four in the morning by now. I didn't feel like praying.

I recall vaguely something about Brigham Young sometimes having to talk himself into prayer when he wasn't in the mood but needed it. It is said he would say something to the effect, "Brigham! It's time to pray."

"I don't feel like praying!" he would answer.

"Brigham! Kneel down and talk to your Heavenly Father!"

"No!"

"*Brigham!*"

"All right, I'll kneel down, but I won't bow my head!"

"Brigham, kneel down and bow your head!"

"No!"

"Brigham!"

"All right, I'll kneel down and bow my head, but I won't close my eyes!"

"Brigham Young, close your eyes!"

"No!"

"Brigham!"

"All right, I'll close my eyes, but I'm not going to say anything!"

"Brigham Young, you close your eyes, and talk to the Lord!"

"No!"

"*BRIGHAM!!*"

93

"Heavenly Father, this is Brigham Young . . ."

Well, I wasn't quite as experienced as Brigham Young, but the idea was similar. I looked around, still a little afraid that someone might see me kneeling out there, and settled for just bowing my head. I suppose this was one of my first really self-initiated communications with the Lord. I remember it was short and to the point, asking sincerely for some kind of intervention.

I knew well that there would, more than likely, not be a personal appearance of an angel with a wrench in his hand, but I suddenly felt something especially good and right about the whole idea of turning to the Lord about a mechanical problem—about *any* problem. A nice feeling began to come over me as I talked the matter over with him. I explained how much the car show meant to me. I felt that I was actually speaking and being heard, that I was being understood by my heavenly friend, even my Father. It was a good feeling.

Following our talk, I returned to the garage and took the flashlight nearby and sought the whereabouts of my recently flying wrench. I found it in the far corner of the garage. I then took my now very familiar stance over the drive line of the car, through the opening of the floorboards, and began again. I took the band in my hand, as I had done so many times previously, and began to slip it into the opening of the transmission. It went down into the transmission just as it had been doing for some eleven hours, and I waited for it as it again began to come out the other side. Right about now is when it would suddenly jump over to the other side, preventing the completion of the assembly; but it didn't! It continued up its precarious course, slowly making its way to the top. I began shaking nervously, watching it come up. I held my breath. It came right up and just sat there, correctly in place, awaiting the assembly of the spring, nut, and bolt.

I found it very difficult to believe my eyes. I was doing nothing different than before; in fact I was much more tired and inaccurate. I took the spring, nut, and bolt and placed them in position. There the finished job stood, almost defiantly. My whole spirit radiated with warm surprise. It had been an actual mechanical answer to a prayer. That day a boy had walked into the garage. That night, a great deal more man walked out. I had tasted deeply of a sweet cup. The experience is dear to me even to this day, as it bears solemn witness to what Alma bore record of. "In *all* thy doings," said he.

If you recognize too much distance between you and your Father, may I offer two additional challenges for help. Number one: Introduce in your life the concept, "Keep your account paid up with the Lord." This is done by living every possible commandment and doing good in every possible way, then pretending the relationship with Heavenly Father is something like a bank checking account. Each good deed and worthiness is a payment on your account. The more you pay in, the more you build up, and the more you can draw out at any time, for *any* worthy cause. "Keep your account paid up with the Lord."

Number two: Take three small file cards, about four by five or five by seven inches. On one of the cards write "BE MASTER"; on the second "THINK FIRST!"; on the third, "WHAT WOULD JESUS DO?" Now place these cards right over the door of your bedroom or in some other conspicuous place where you will see them each time you leave home to join society with its many temptations to do wrong. Apply the satisfying character trait of self-discipline, together with the other six keys to happiness which we have discussed, and congratulations on your new happiness and better, closer relationship with your Heavenly Father. If discouragement sneaks in, don't give up. Try again, and again.

And so, at the close of this writing, may I bear my solemn witness about these things spoken. They work; I have tried them. *When conscientiously and honestly applied*, they endow one with greater happi-

95

ness. God lives. I bear testimony of this sacred fact. We are here voluntarily upon this earth to be tested. Make it a happy experience, a joyful eternal memory. In his Son's holy name, even Jesus Christ. Amen.